COSMIC PURPOSE
and
HUMAN CONSCIOUSNESS

COSMIC PURPOSE
and
HUMAN CONSCIOUSNESS

Richard A. Mould

RESOURCE *Publications* • Eugene, Oregon

COSMIC PURPOSE AND HUMAN CONSCIOUSNESS

Resource Publications
An Imprint of Wipf and Stock Publishers
199 W. 8th Ave., Suite 3
Eugene, OR 97401

www.wipfandstock.com

ISBN 13: 978-1-4982-3147-3

Manufactured in the U.S.A.   11/09/2015

CONTENTS

———

ILLUSTRATIONS

PREFACE

YOU MAY FEEL OVERWHELMED by the gigantic universe that is revealed by astronomy, not to mention the curious quantum world
that lies beneath your gaze All of this may make you feel unim-
portant and insignificant. But that is far from true. You are in fact
on the *leading edge* of the evolution of the universe.

The universe evolved in a very mechanical way for billions of
years, eventually producing living organisms of a robotic nature.
And then consciousness was introduced. We don't know when that
happened, but many believe that it occurred with the introduction
of new mammalian forms after the mass extinction 65 million
years ago. Be that as it may, the universe at that point made an
unbelievable transition: It became aware of itself. For the first time
the universe was able to experience its own movements and to see
its own landscapes. For the first time the universe was able to feel
emotions, to go hungry, and to engage in internecine combat. For
the first time the universe made an effort to understand itself, and
in the end, it asked penetrating questions about itself. The universe
became conscious and curious about its new experiences.

What is the purpose of the universe? This book is devoted to
answering that question. But however it is answered, the coming to
consciousness is pivotal to any believable narrative. This innovation has evolved to the advanced form that we see in ourselves,
giving humans the most highly developed consciousness that exists in this part of the universe It places us at the apex of whatever

the universe has in mind. So as a human you are very important to creation's purpose. In fact, you are essential to the point of it all.

However one defines cosmic purpose, it is essential to recognize that the universe is a fusion of quantitative and qualitative realities. Every conscious experience bears this out. No one has ever had a qualitative experience by itself without a qualitative complement, and vice versa. Observation always has these inseparable parts—a dualism that we experience in nature; or at least, a dualism that we are able to read into nature.

All of nature is of course monistic, but we humans separate it into quantitative and qualitative parts for the purpose of analysis. Science has focused on the quantitative part, constructing an enormously impressive objective universe. Since that construction does not include the qualitative part, many conclude that qualitative experience is unreal—that it's some kind of illusion. But that ignores half of experienced reality.

The quantitative and qualitative experiences together make up our individual subjective experience, and I call that sum our *subjective world*. Our quantitative experiences by themselves will be called our *objective world* from which science has constructed a theoretical *objective universe*. Symmetry suggests that the subjective world should also be expanded into a *subjective universe*—a hypothetical subjective construction of universal extent. That is done in the following pages. I'm convinced that the resulting subjective universe is an essential "other side" of the objective universe, and that the two together are necessary to explain the whole of our experiences. The resulting "universes" are understood to be the causes of the two experienced "worlds".

There are now four parts to the universe: The objective and subjective worlds of individual experience, and the objective and subjective universes that are theoretical generalizations of those two worlds. These four are diagrammed in chapter 6 showing how they are related to each other, and how new forces must be introduced to account for the claimed influence of consciousness. Physics does not now recognize forces of this kind, but that is only because physics hasn't yet recognized consciousness itself, or its influence in the universe.

Purpose is not just a subjective property of individuals. In the universe that we've constructed, purpose can also exist within the subjective universe apart from individuals, giving purpose a cosmic reach. It is the intent of this book to explore that reach. We find that there are many attainable cosmic purposes within the subjective universe, all hypothetical possibilities, but we restrict attention to a minimal formulation that has implications for progressive developments in human history. In subsequent chapters we look for evidence of this purposeful influence.

That purpose is in evidence in a historic survey in Part II. The human race has experienced a great deal of social, economic, political, and religious progress in recent millennia—all positive purposeful developments; although in this book we only cite cases in the West since medieval times. Progressive ideas in these areas have been most notable in recent centuries, but the advance is not linear. We go two steps forward and one step backward. I document this uneven evolution showing that social and religious progress in the West is positive at the moment, although we have fallen on economic and political hard times in recent years.

The book deals with religious matters but it does not discuss traditional claims concerning God or revealed truth. In his "Leviathan," Thomas Hobbes describes a sovereign whose authority is based on the violence-prone characteristics of its subjects, rather than on *divine right*—a novel innovation for the mid-seventeenth century.[1] In this book I describe a "cosmic purpose" whose origins are based on the characteristics of humans in an objective/subjective universe, rather than on a *divine being*—a novel innovation for our time.

The introduction of consciousness into the universe was an essential turning point in its evolution, and we humans are the most advanced manifestation of consciousness in this part of the universe. We are the frontier of the universe because *we are*

1. Hobbes, *Leviathan*.

its self-awareness. Without us the universe would be barren and pointless; but through you and me the universe is alive—observing and thinking and feeling—and divining purpose.

PART I

1

TWO WORLDS

It is commonly assumed that the objective world around us is real and that the subjective world of the individual is illusion. In this chapter both worlds are found to be equally real. They are two sides of the same coin.

COMMON SENSE OBJECTIVITY

The objective world is commonly understood to include tables, chairs, and automobiles. It is the collection of all the things that populate a person's life. From video games to poplar trees, objective reality is the sum of all the things that we find in our surroundings. For most people this includes the sensed properties of things. An apple is red, a whistle is loud and shrill, rotten eggs smell bad, and the bark of a tree is rough to the touch. There may be some ambiguity on this point because different people may sense things differently, but for the most part people take colors, odors, sounds, and the felt properties of things to be part of the objective world that they inhabit.

COMMON SENSE SUBJECTIVITY

The subjective world is commonly understood to include the personal things that we experience. Our private thoughts and emotions are part of the subjective world that we live in by ourselves. We may project our thoughts and emotions onto others and satisfy ourselves that we know and understand someone else's inner self; but basically we are alone in our own subjective world, struggling to get along with others who live alone in their subjective worlds. We do not believe ourselves to be alone in the objective world that we share with others.

Common sense reality is a combination of these two worlds. It is a conflicted merger of these different aspects of our experience. The objective world is thought to be identical with a universe that exists with or without someone around to verify its existence; and the subjective world is thought to be something that came into the objective world accompanying conscious beings, where one of these worlds is not reducible to the other. The objective world does not have thoughts and emotions like a conscious being, and a conscious being does not have rigid predictability like objects in the objective world. Matter and energy are conserved in the objective world. They may change their form but they are never entirely created or destroyed; whereas the thoughts and emotions of conscious beings come and go with baffling irregularity. In the end, subjectivity dies and objectivity persists. There is a commonly held belief that objectivity is a stable reality and that subjectivity is a fleeting illusion.

ANOTHER WAY

There is another more precise way to understand the above distinction. Begin with the *experienced world* of the individual. That world is an overlay of quantitative and qualitative features. The quantitative parts are the measurable parts of one's experience that are reducible to the meters, kilograms, and seconds of Newtonian mechanics. This is the part that scientists abstract from direct experience to give each his own *objective world*. When they enter their laboratories scientists tend to ignore the purely private parts of their experience and turn their attention to the quantities that can be measured and reported as empirical evidence.

On the other hand, it is also possible for a person to focus on the purely qualitative aspects of experience like immediate sensations, feelings, and emotions. When these properties are abstracted from the experienced world the result is the *subjective world of the individual*. At this stage we say that the subjective world does not include everything in a person's private life. It includes sensations such as sights and sounds, tastes and smells, and it includes emotional states such as happy or sad, but it does not include memories, instincts, or ideas. These are temporarily excluded so we can focus attention on "direct and immediate" experience. Therefore, the subjective world (as temporarily defined) is a snapshot of the impressions that come from the environment at a given moment of time, plus the person's emotional state at that moment.

It follows that our senses are *entirely* subjective. This is different from the common sense distinction at the beginning of the chapter. As previously stated, common sense tells us that the colors, tastes, and odors are the properties of the things in our surroundings, with the caveat that different people may experience them somewhat differently. This is now modified to place *all* sensations (all colors, tastes, and odors) inside of our subjective selves.

We now have three distinctions: There is (1) the *experienced world* of the individual, (2) the *objective world* that is abstracted from the quantitative part of the experienced world, and (3) the *subjective world* that is another name for our awareness of both parts of the experienced world—the quantitative parts and the qualitative parts. We attach importance to the objective-subjective division because of the great success of science in clarifying and dealing with the objective part.

The question is: how should we assign reality to each of these distinctions? This is a philosophical question that you are free to answer as you please. You may say that all of them are real or all are illusion or some combination is real or illusion. However, this book makes a definite commitment on the matter of reality at this level.

I begin this book with the assertion that the 'experienced world' is the basic reality. It is the ontological anchor on which all other realities are attached. It is the beginning of everything that anyone is likely to take seriously enough to call "real." I next say that both the quantitative and the qualitative aspects of that experience are equally real. There is no reason to say that an abstraction in one direction is real and that an abstraction in the other direction is an illusion. There is an ontological symmetry here that seems to forbid a biased preference one way or the other. The quantitative world and the qualitative world of the individual are complementary realities. They are two sides of a single coin and they share the reality of the coin. Why, after all, would the universe present itself as part real and part illusion?

If you see a red apple you observe that it has a shape that is quantifiable, so its shape is a property of your objective world. You also observe that it has a quality of redness that you say is a property of your subjective world. We say here that reality is attached to its objective shape and equally to its subjective color, for there is no basis *in the experience* to assign reality to one and not the other. They appear together in a mutually supportive way.

Importance is often given to the fact that the objective world is defined in a publically verifiable way and that the subjective world is private. It is therefore concluded by many that the subjective world must be an illusion. It's true that everyone agrees as to the shape of the apple and that each may see a slightly different color. It's true that the shape is understood to be independent of observation, and that its color emerges out of an interaction between the apple's light and the observer. These are valid distinctions but *they are not ontological distinctions*. The light coming from the apple is real and the interaction between the light and the observer is real, so the thing that emerges from that interaction is also real. There is no reason to believe otherwise. If the color you see is different from the color that another person sees, then your interactive systems must be different. That does not mean that the product of the interactions in either case is an illusion.

You can think of an apple as being red *or* you can think of it as sending you photons of a certain wavelength, and your world does not come crashing down in dualistic disharmony. That's because there is no point in your experienced world at which these two understandings directly collide. If you look at an interference pattern you see the lines that measure wavelength; and simultaneously, you see the color of the light that makes up the pattern. There is no conflict. Both color and pattern are equally present in the experience, so they are separate but equal phenomena. Of course two different people might see slightly different shades of color because their brains are slightly different, so they call up slightly different images. However, each one experiences both color and pattern. There is no reason for either one of them to downgrade any part of their own experience.

A possible asymmetry lies in the scientific claim that objectivity explains everything whereas subjectivity explains very little, and therefore objectivity rules. However, we will show in the following chapters that certain physical forces also appear in conjunction with subjective states. In chapter 4 we identify *anchor forces* that accompany emotional states such as pleasure or pain; and we identify *nonanchor forces* in chapter 6, that accompany information gathering experiences like sight or sound. Physics does not now include these forces among the fundamental four, but I say that they are nonetheless necessarily. They are essential to understanding consciousness, so contemporary physics is incomplete without them. Completion will be possible only when physics has understood the intricacies of conscious creatures and their novel internal forces, thereby giving subjectivity a comparable status with objectivity as a source of natural forces.

IRRECONCILABLE DIFFERENCES

In the case of an apple and most other objects of experience, there is an easy compatibility between the quantitative and the qualitative worlds. However, there are areas of apparent conflict that seem to be irreconcilable as between *determinism* and *free-will.*

The immediate cause of any particular action appears to be a desire to act. However, scientifically speaking, that desire is due to something else, and that in turn is due to something else, and so on. A person may experience the desire and maybe the first something else, and even the second something else, but experience is limited. It does not go as far as the scientific understanding that says: The causal sequence reduces to biochemical and neurological causes that further reduce to atomic and subatomic causes. This is the scientific or deterministic account of why people do what they do.

On the other hand, subjectively speaking, one's action is entirely caused by directly experienced desire. There may be things in the environment or in the body that are factors in that decision, but the individual is *the ultimate decider* concerning the weight of those factors. This is the personal or free-will account of why people do what people do.

The experience itself offers both interpretations—the quantitative and the qualitative. There is nothing in experience that gives an ontological edge to one or the other. *Every one of your decision-making experiences is neutral concerning how that decision is made.* You may believe that the decision is causally based on your desires, or you may believe that it is causally based on something beyond those desires. You may abstract free-will from the experience, or you may abstract determinism from that same experience; but the experience itself does not exclude either one and it allows both. That's because *raw experience itself says nothing about cause.* You provide the "cause" by organizing the experience in such a way as to explain it to yourself.

THE OTHER WOMAN

There is a simple line drawing shown in figure 1 that can be seen in two entirely different ways. Looking at it one way you see the image of a beautiful young woman. She is looking to her right so you see her left profile with her left jaw line and earlobe clearly indicated. She has dark hair and is wearing a heavy dark coat with a white hood. In the other way of looking at the sketch you see an old woman with a large nose. She wears the same black coat with a white hood and is looking down and to the left. The young woman's left ear is now the old woman's left eye, the young woman's necklace is now the old woman's mouth, and the young woman's left cheek is now the old woman's nose.

Figure 1. The other Woman
Called: "A New Ambiguous Figure"
in *American Journal of Psychology*
42.3 (July 1930) 444–445

You may at first have difficulty flipping from one of these images to the other, but in time you will learn to go back and forth with ease. These images are called *gestalts*. A gestalt is *a way of organizing information that results in an intelligible or recognizable pattern.* This term not only applies to line drawings but to any kind of raw data or information.

For instance, two economists might interpret the nations economic data differently: maybe one from the perspective of capitalism and the other from the perspective of socialism. They see the same facts differently, and they arrive at different conclusions. We say that their brains form opposing gestalts. That is: They find different ways to organize the given economic information so as to make it intelligible to themselves.

Also, two senators on different sides of the aisle will look at the same political facts and draw entirely different conclusions. Again, we say that their brains form different gestalts. They find different ways of organizing the facts so as to make them intelligible to themselves and to their partisan colleagues.

Evidently social information can be organized into recognizable social gestalts or beliefs, economic data can be organized into familiar economic gestalts or theories, political particulars can be organized into preferred political gestalts or ideologies, and religious experience can be organized into satisfying religious gestalts or faiths. These gestalts represent *different ways of looking at a subject matter*. The brain assembles information one way or another depending on belief, or on theory, or ideology, or faith; or perhaps it depends alone on simple preference. In the case of the above line drawing the choice may seem to be randomly determined, whereas social, economic, political, and religious gestalts usually involve a long history of information gathering and assimilation. For many, the choice is frequently a matter of common sense.

Experience alone is free of interpretations, just as the above line drawing by itself is free of interpretations. The contradictory images of the young woman and the old woman appear only when an observer enters the picture. *It is only when one organizes experience into opposing gestalts that conflicting ideas are created*. That conflict does not exist at the level of naked experience. It emerges when a decider attempts to "understand" the source of his decisions.

Question: How can both determinism and free-will be correct when they so blatantly contradict one another? **Answer**: Remember, they are different interpretations of raw data—data that is itself without contradiction. In this case the data comes directly from the experienced world so the resulting gestalts are not only equally valid, they are *equally valid interpretations of reality*.

Social, economic, political, and religious gestalts are flexible on the matter of their reality, and like most people I have definite preferences among them. I attach a reality to some gestalts and not to others because I may consider those others to be naive, heavy-handed, or even malicious. Nonetheless, *I insist on neutrality* between the above "quantitative" and "qualitative" gestalts for the reason that they are ubiquitous at the most fundamental level of our experience, and because it is bizarre to suppose that the universe reifies one part of itself but not the other. The conclusions of this book depend on accepting the ontological parity of quantitative and subjective qualitative gestalts.

Scientists do not generally agree with this characterization. They agree that free-will and color are confined to the subjective world but they regard them both as illusions. But why would the universe present us with illusions? Why would the universe create an illusion that exists side-by-side with a dominant reality? It is more likely that the universe expanded reality the moment it introduced consciousness, and that we are the ones who call consciousness an illusion because we haven't yet figured out what it is. We haven't been able to find its relationship to science. And that is the problem. *We fail to see the reality of our own consciousness inasmuch as we have failed (so far) to integrate it into our scientific understanding of things.* We have so far failed to recognize the anchor and nonanchor forces that are associated with consciousness. This failure is due to the fact that physics has not fully investigated the conscious organisms that display these forces, for they are the most complicated systems that exist in the known universe. The oversight is therefore understandable. However, it is proposed in these pages that the arguments presented in chapter 4 (where the influence of anchor forces is first recognized) and in chapter 6 (where nonanchor forces are first introduced) are sufficient to establish the existence of these forces beyond the fundamental four that are now known to physics.

SUMMARY

The two worlds we speak of in this chapter concern the dualism of experience when it is separated into quantitative and qualitative parts. That is illustrated by the above color vs. the shape, and color vs. wavelength dichotomies. The naked experience in these cases is fully monistic and represents a basic reality. The strange thing is that many people split these experiences into real and imaginary parts. This chapter claims that that is an arbitrary and unjustified separation. You see the colors red and green and you are part of the universe. Therefore, red and green are part of the universe.

Nature presents us with experiences that are real and of one piece. It is useful for many reasons to split those experiences into quantitative parts (called objective) and qualitative parts (called subjective), *but it is absurd for us to redistribute the reality of those parts—giving special favor to one over the other.* It is concluded that the quantitative and qualitative worlds of our experience are equally real. They share the reality of the underlying whole.

Question: Doesn't probability in quantum mechanics, and Heisenberg's uncertainty principle in particular, imply that free-will is operating at the fundamental level of our objective universe? **Answer**: No! Quantum probability is a causally determined variable just as it is in classical mechanics. If a coin is tossed in the air 1000 times it will generally come down "heads" close to 500 times. This does not mean that the coin has free-will. If it did have free-will it might choose to come down heads 900 times out of 1000 *as often as it pleases*. But it doesn't do that. *It can't do that.* The coin isn't free to make decisions of that kind. The probability of its coming down heads or tails is determined by the rigidly determined *laws of probability*. The same is true of quantum probability applied to quantum mechanical particles.

On the other hand, free-will is an attribute of the qualitative part of experience. It has properties of its own that are entirely independent of the quantitative (i.e., objective scientific) aspect of experience.

2

MISTAKES PEOPLE MAKE

──────────

ONE OF THE FIRST mistakes of humans is the belief that they are objectively capable of *owning things*. Ownership is an infantile illusion that we grown-ups turn into a legal principle. It is not simply a desire to control. Ownership involves the gathering of our many things into a fictitious bundle that we believe is exclusively our own. This chapter explores the ramifications of the idea of ownership and of its denial. It is claimed here that no part of the objective universe can own any other part ; and since humans are part of the universe, we cannot own anything at all. Our worldly estate is objectively non-existent in principle. Only the universe as a whole can be said to be the proprietor of its contents.

OBJECTIVE OWNERSHIP

The land that I own is a slice of the wider universe that I pretend belongs to me in some personal way. The state encourages this illusion and further claims sovereignty over me and my property. Ownership and sovereignty are social fictions that we create in order to keep the peace. Primitive societies do not generally allow its members to own land, preferring a more communal arrangement, but they fiercely reserve rights of sovereignty. The tribe is typically territorial as are the many rivals it keeps at bay.

Taken to its logical conclusion, it follows that when American astronauts planted the flag on the moon, America thereafter owned the moon. I do not think anyone at NASA or Washington actually made that claim, but I am a little surprised that they didn't; for I'm sure that many Americans felt that way about the lunar conquest. Newt Gingrich wants the make the moon the 51st state. Americans have every reason to be proud of the achievement but we have no claim to lunar ownership. None of us own any part of nature, either as individuals, or as tribes, or as nations.

It is uncertain how far up into the sky our estate is supposed to go or how far down into the ground. For the most part we don't give these things much thought because we are primarily concerned with the earth's surface where we live out our lives. The title to our land is measured in acres. However, if we could do so we would no doubt follow the instincts of our infantile past and make a grab for whatever is above us and below us. The trouble is, we don't know where in the sky to plant our territorial flags, or how to stake out a claim in the earth below.

The accumulators among us are especially mindful of what they possess. These are the ones for whom ownership is an end in itself. Wealthy individuals are often wedded to extensive ownership because of the power it gives them, or because of the control, or influence it gives them. Or perhaps they are tantalized by the envy they inspire due to their vast possessions. However, these motivations are not the issue. The accumulators are people who pursue ownership as such, independent of other perks. These are the ones for whom ownership is its own reward. These are the ones who have carried the infantile fear of separation to its fullest expression.

If gathering things onto one's self is what most people mean by ownership, then this would have little meaning if the *self* were not also owned. The proprietor of material things is also assumed to be owned by the owner. Otherwise there is no point. It makes no sense to say that a robot owns the clothing it wears, for we do not think of a robot as an owner. To say that you are capable of owning your clothing is to say that you have rights of ownership. Unlike a robot, you supposedly have a claim on the proprietorial center of activity that is yourself. You own yourself to begin with, and that is how you come to own other things.

This is the first mistake: *The belief that a person is the (objective) proprietor of himself and his toys.* In reality, there is no such thing as objective ownership by any part of nature short of the universe itself. Different parts of the universe may specialize in some way, thereby differentiating themselves from other parts, but a subdivision of the objective universe for proprietary purposes is artificial and illusory.

SUBJECTIVE EGO

The ego is the individual's own bundle of ownership. It is a part of the *subjective world* and is equal to a totality of the physical and psychological self-images to which one is attached. It includes a self-defining account of one's physical and psychological development, and a catalog of failures and successes along the way. However characterized, ego is a partisan advocate of the subjective self. It is each person's dog in the fight. Without a sturdy ego, the individual would be unable to function in a world that would otherwise disable him.

Freud gave the ego a dynamical role in his theory of human behavior that performs at the unconscious level as well as the conscious level. In this book however, ego will refer only to the above conscious package of identifying characteristics, independent of any role it might play in a psychological theory. We will only consider the conscious ego that regards itself as a center of ownership. We will say that ego is: *the proprietary core of the conscious individual* that draws the self together with whatever else it can appropriate. It is a bundle that belongs to each individual's subjective world.

SOUL

While the ego can be given a more-or-less accurate description, the "soul" of religious tradition is a part of the subjective world that has a more ethereal nature. It is an extension of ego that is said to persist when the physical body no longer exists. The soul continues to exist after the physiological and psychological body has been destroyed and other possessions have been redistributed to heirs. This notion of soul is a creation of humans that is intended to extend the ego beyond the grave. The ego does not want to die. It therefore gathers itself into a transcendental essence that supposedly lives forever.

A stripped down version of the soul often loses many of the possessions of its current ego, particularly the undesirable ones. The soul that enters heaven is presumed to be "a soul of virtue." We hang onto the things about ourselves that we prize, and jettison those we would rather not acknowledge. We believe that the essential soul is good. Some people go further to divest their souls of almost all of its familiar features. They say they were someone else in a previous life and expect to be someone else in a future life. They take on different characteristics at different times but they somehow preserve the same soul. The soul is distilled to almost invisible essentials that are the essence of the person. Objectively speaking, all these scenarios are fairy tales that we tell ourselves because we want to participate in the everlasting.

On the other hand, conscious creatures make good use of ego. It unifies subjective purpose, action, and intent. One would have difficulty surviving without a strong and gainfully employed ego that aids in one's defense and charts a successful course through life. The cosmos is well served when its creatures possess well-developed egos. So the health of the ego, like the lung and the liver, is central to the health of the individual. And like the lung and the liver, ego serves no purpose when the organism is no longer alive. As the body goes to dust, so does the psychological self that is held together by ego; and in the end, a transcendent ego (a soul) serves no purpose and does not exist.

SEPARATION

We have seen that humans mistakenly take possession of things in order to deal with the anxiety of separation, but the prior mistake is separation itself. We see ourselves as apart from the universe. We are of course "a part of" but we are not "apart from" the great cosmos. Each of us is a single center of awareness in a universe that is full of such centers.

Great achievers tend to look to their achievements as exclusively their own. They tend to separate their "empire" from everything else in the universe, giving it a special status. It's that part of the universe that they supposedly built by themselves. As Mr. Successful looks out from the 60th floor of his tower, surveying the limits of his domain, he gives himself full credit for its creation. He believes he did it all himself.

However, where was Mr. Successful when the planet was being formed out of the dust of a supernova? Where was he when water filled the oceans? Where was he when biological systems were evolving over a billion-year history? Where was he when the land was cleared and highways were built? Where was he when laborers carried mortar and steel to the 60th floor? Mr. Successful may have played a role in the final stages of all that but, objectively speaking, it was a limited role. He could never have done it without the universe that made it possible and without all those other humans who did their share.

There it is again! One should not say the universe *and* other humans, as though they are two different things. How easy it is to fall into the separation trap. Humans are of course part of the universe so the last sentence should read: He (Mr. Successful) could never have done it without *all* the parts of the universe that contributed to making that 60-story tower. Look around you! The building that you occupy (or are looking at) was constructed by the universe. It is true that the universe used humans to accomplish that feat, but objectively speaking, humans are little more than robots that were built by the universe for the purpose of making towers. Objectively speaking there is no free-will so it was not Mr.

Successful that willed or could have willed anything of the kind. Surely it is valid to speak of the achievements of mankind where that means the achievements of that part of the universe that we call mankind. However, there is no reason to make much of this distinction. The planets, the oceans, the land, and all the creatures that wonder over the land are part of a single story: a universe that is fulfilling its own destiny.

Subjectively speaking the message is of course different. From that point of view we separate ourselves from the rest of the world through our egos and we take possession of the things we gather around us for good reason. We exercise our free-will to insure that our ego, our body, and all of our apparent possessions are well tended and well defended. It is thorough the subjectively understood ego that we are given the wherewithal to survive as stable organisms in a world that would otherwise tear us apart.. Objectively, the ego is a fool's fabrication. Subjectively, it is an essential edifice of the individual. Both of these conflicted understandings are equally valid within their own objective or subjective gestalts.

3

THE SUBJECTIVE
UNIVERSE

THE SCIENTIST, WORKING WITHIN his own objective world, generalizes his results using mathematics and logic. He expands his findings far beyond himself to create a vast and marvelous model of the universe as a whole. It will be called the *objective universe* (as opposed to the scientist's own objective world). This creation of science is not directly experienced. It begins with an abstraction from experience (i.e., the quantitative part) and builds from there to go beyond anything that anyone knows about empirically. It is a theory, a construct of the mind. It imagines a universe that existed before there were conscious creatures, or planets, or stars. It goes all the way back to the Big Bang that no one has directly experienced, and all the way down to elementary particles that no one has directly seen. Even at the level of the familiar pool table, the objective universe is a theory. It is an abstraction from the experienced world.

This universe began its expansion thirteen or fourteen billion years ago. It created the physical and chemical environment that enabled an extensive biological development. It created living organisms that were mere robots, and finally it created conscious organisms. That entire evolution is remarkable, but with the introduction of consciousness, the universe made an unbelievable transition: It became aware of itself.

It did this by first creating special configurations of matter (i.e., brains) that are able to receive or reflect consciousness. The term "reflect" is preferred because it permits an easy analogy with crystals. On the face of it, the redness of a ruby appears to be a property of the gem, but it is only a reflection of a more ambient thing. The ruby is a facilitator of redness, not an originator. In a similar way, brains are facilitators of consciousness but they are not the originators of consciousness.

In this chapter we imagine an assembly of all possible aspects of experience into a hypothetical body that we call the *subjective universe* (as distinguished from the subjective world). We then endow this body with powers of its own: it becomes that which is reflected by brains. Initially defined *by* consciousness, the subjective universe is finally presumed to be *the cause of* consciousness—analogous to the way things are done on the objective side

REFLECTED CONSCIOUSNESS

A ruby is red because ambient radiation of the right frequency is reflected by its crystalline structure. The spacing of the molecules inside the ruby and the ability of these molecules to scatter light provide the necessary conditions to reflect red light. Redness is therefore a property of the ambient light that is reflected by the ruby; so the light that is observed by someone looking at the crystal is not the crystal's light. A ruby is not itself red.

Similarly, the brain of a conscious creature has an *ability to reflect consciousness.* By virtue of the structure of its parts (i.e., configurations of neurons, ions, and receptors) the brain processes conscious experiences; where the thing that is processed is not intrinsic to the brain. Consciousness does not exist between the molecules of the brain, bursting forth when called upon—no more than red light exists between the molecules of a ruby, bursting forth when called upon.

It is through brains that particular aspects of consciousness resonate. One configuration of brain parts will reflect sadness. Another configuration will reflect anger. Still another will reflect a shiny light or a loud noise. A brain filters out particular components of the complete spectrum of consciousness that somehow resides in the wider universe. The brain resonates with particular states of consciousness depending on how its parts are configured.

The question then is: where does reflected consciousness come from? There is no ambient "objective substance" that is the source of consciousness, so it must originate in a wider non-objective feature of the universe. But where? Where do shoulder pains come from? Where do fears of failure or distressing thoughts originate? You may have these thoughts and experiences but they come from another part of the universe. They are yours to enjoy or endure but they originate somewhere else.

THE SUBJECTIVE UNIVERSE

We construct a *subjective universe* that is assumed to have existed before conscious creatures existed, accompanying the objective universe from the time of the Big Bang. We will say that before brains existed, the subjective part of the universe was completely *undifferentiated*—its parts were completely indistinguishable. The universe did not (at this time) experience things. It did not become conscious of particular things (like landscapes or moving objects) until brains came along to process those images. Currently, the subjective universe continues to harbor undifferentiated forms of consciousness, but it also includes *differentiated* (i.e., distinguishable) forms that have interacted with brain structure.

The subjective world of chapter 1 was said to exclude all memories, instincts, and ideas; however, both the subjective world and the subjective universe will now be understood to include the full range of possible experiences. The four parts of experienced and theoretical reality are related to each other in figure 2. The full universe is a fusion of these four parts, making a unified whole.

Abstracted from experience   Theoretical extension

Objective World   ⇒←   Objective Universe

              ←

Subjective World   ⇒←   Subjective Universe

Figure 2: Four parts of the universe and their connections

The double-headed arrow –» in the top row in figure 2 indicates that the objective universe is initially constructed from observations in the objective world. The left-going arrow in the top row indicates that the objective world is understood to be a causal consequence of the objective universe. The former is derived from the latter. Scientists believe that the determinism we experience in our objective world is an instance of the determinism of the hypothesized objective universe.

The double-headed arrow –» in the bottom row going from the subjective world to the subjective universe indicates that the latter is also a theoretical construction. This universe includes all conscious forms that together stand side-by-side with the objective universe. It was previously imagined that our subjective world is a reflection of a wider reality, and we now suppose that the undifferentiated subjective universe *is* that wider reality. It is the source of brain reflected consciousness indicated by the left-going arrow in the bottom row plus the angled arrow going from the subjective universe to the objective world. The differentiated part of the subjective universe covers the experienced worlds of the individual..[1]

John Locke says, "It is . . . repugnant to the idea of senseless matter that it should put into itself sense, perception, and knowledge. . . . " Therefore, senseless matter can only be given these qualities by an agent *outside of itself.* That agent for Locke is a

---

1. The subjective universe in figure 2 can be thought of as just the undifferentiated part of consciousness. The complete subjective universe includes that, plus the differentiated conscious part that covers both the objective and the subjective worlds.

supernatural God. In this book, that agent is the natural subjective universe that reflects sense, perception, and knowledge through the senseless matter of the brain.[2]

Question: Does the subjective universe exist everywhere, together with the objective universe? **Answer**: Yes! The total universe is just one thing—an inseparable amalgam of quantitative and qualitative parts. So where the objective universe exists, the subjective universe exists as well.

Question: Was the universe conscious before there were brains in the universe? **Answer**: No! This is the old question: does the tree that falls in the forest make a noise if no one is around to hear it? The answer is: the tree makes sound waves but no noise. Similarly, before there were brains in the universe, undifferentiated consciousness existed in the subjective universe, but it was not *experienced* by the universe. No thing in the pre-conscious universe (such as a falling rock) produced a noise.

Nonanchor forces are not indicated in figure 2. They will be included in later chapters where we discuss the nature of each of these forces. The four forces currently known to physics are also not indicated. They are implicitly contained in the objective universe, and their effects are observed in the objective world of the individual.

Consciousness does not originate in the brain any more than red originates in the ruby. It is also true that conscious experience is never *located* in the brain of the observer. The brain is the major processing site of conscious experience but it is not the "manifestation site." You experience emotions throughout your body but not in your brain. You experience a pain in your toe—*in your toe*. You do not experience it in your brain. You don't even experience a headache in your brain; but rather, it is located in the muscles that surround your skull. Furthermore, you have sight and sound experiences that are completely "outside" of your body. You see

2. Locke, *Essays Concerning*, 100–101.

someone sitting in a chair *across the room*. You do not see that person sitting in a chair in your brain. The brain is not equipped to experience things directly. It only processes, or reflects, conscious experiences that appear elsewhere. Your subjective world is therefore a phenomenon that is located at different sites throughout your body and in regions of space outside of your body, fully apart from the processing centers in your brain. This is foreign to the common understanding, but it's a fact. For centuries people had no idea what the brain was for or what it did. Aristotle thought that the brain was a secondary organ that acted as a cooling agent for the blood. The Egyptians thought that emotion and wisdom were centered in the heart. That's because humans are not directly aware of the brain or any of its functions. All of your emotional experiences are located in parts of you body other than your brain; and your experiences of most "things" are located completely outside of your body.

Consciousness *originates* in the subjective universe. It is *processed* in the brain, and it *manifests* itself somewhere else—in violation of common sense and the present scientific paradigm. This strange feature of consciousness violates the notion of "contiguous cause"; for unlike contemporary causal influences, the manifestation of consciousness appears some distance away from its processing site. There is a "gap" between the processing site of consciousness in the brain, and the manifestation site of conscious experience. That alone presents a challenge to contemporary science.

Therefore, science must make a significant leap in a new direction if it is to include consciousness in its findings. We await that understanding as well as a scientific recognition of the anchor and nonanchor forces that are associated with consciousness.

In summary, the "subjective universe" is a hypothesis like the objective universe of science. It is the sum of all of our *differentiated* experiences including the sound of every bell and the thought of every Spring—plus the *undifferentiated* forms of consciousness that have not yet been filtered through the brain. When the (undifferentiated) subjective universe passes through the brain it is the cause of all forms of (differentiated) subjective experience; similar to the way the objective universe is the cause of objective experience. The objective and subjective universes are both necessary to fully explain our experiences in the universe.

4

FIRST CAUSE[1]

IT WAS CLAIMED IN previous chapters that the introduction of consciousness requires two new forces that must be added to the fundamental four that are currently known in physics. The first is the "anchor force" that is associated with feelings and emotions; and the second is the "nonanchor force" that is associated primarily with sight and sound. This chapter is devoted to explaining the need for the first of these—the anchor forces.

For feelings and emotions to evolve in parallel with biology, it is necessary to require that they have a direct causal influence on biology. Unlike ordinary forces in physics, anchor forces must go between conscious elements and physiology, causing both to evolve in parallel with one another. A fully evolved conscious creature is well coordinated in both mind and body, and that would not happen without an interaction that harmonizes the two during the creature's evolution. We conclude this chapter with figure 3 that is a modification of figure 2. It shows the four parts of the universe plus the effects of anchor forces.

---

1. With some alterations this chapter is taken from Mould *Evolution I*.

BACKGROUND

Most physical and biological scientists say that physiological evolution proceeds along mechanical lines only. They claim that the fundamental forces of physics and chemistry combine with chance mutations to select the physiology of a species that will best survive the evolutionary struggle. Consciousness is assumed to have appeared separately. It is understood to have come about through certain physiological configurations (i.e., maybe certain configurations of neurons) and is somehow a byproduct of known fundamental forces. Consciousness, they say, is not itself a force in nature. It cannot cause things to happen. It is influenced *by* physiology, but it cannot have a reciprocal influence *on* physiology, although it appears to do so. That appearance is supposedly an illusion that has no basis in physics. Consciousness, they say, has no place among the fundamental forces, so its imagined influence is a deception.

It is important to recognize the great improbability of this idea: It claims that consciousness has no objective influence and therefore serves no evolutionary purpose. But if something serves no evolutionary purpose it generally *atrophies*; or if it doesn't atrophy, it at least *ossifies*. In any case, it does not continue to evolve in functional parallel with the species, achieving higher and higher forms consistent with and appropriate to the physiological development of the species. For example, an appropriately evolved conscious organism will consciously experience sitting down when its body sits down, and it will consciously experience fear when its body is in physical danger. It would be a miracle if correspondences like that were to occur without good reason—without consciousness being interactively engaged with physiology. If a chance mutation did bring about some unrelated and irrelevant conscious phenomenon, there is no reason to believe that it would persist for centuries, developing in parallel with physiology. It is more likely to stage a pointless display for a time and then disappear for lack of purpose. The idea that an inconsequential illusion will persist over time *and* develop into a reliable mirror of "physical reality" requires an enormous stretch of imagination.

There are several ways that this argument might be stated but it comes down to two basic ideas:

1. Consciousness must have *served an evolutionary purpose* for otherwise it would not have survived. It is simply improbable that evolution would produce and nurture a useless appendage to physiology over an extended period of time.

2. Consciousness is introduced into a species by genetic mutation. It *exercises a causal influence* by shaping the evolutionary development of physiology, and is in turn shaped by physiology.

This general idea was first expressed by William James, who said that the evolution of "appropriate" subjective feelings would be incomprehensible if feelings were biologically redundant.[2]

Many say that consciousness is an illusion that the brain creates, and its existence is basically inexplicable. They say it is an airy essence that shrouds physiology without effect. William Clifford says that *all matter* is accompanied by a rudimentary sentience that flowers into more sophisticated forms of consciousness when matter takes on more sophisticated structural configurations.[3] This is panpsychism, a more recent form of which is discussed by Chalmers.[4] Many in the artificial-intelligence community favor the idea that neurological software alone gives rise to consciousness with no reciprocal consequences.[5] However, these views do not account for the fact that conscious phenomenon so faithfully reflects the environment in which the body participates. They imagine that an otherwise useless consciousness comes into existence *ad hoc* with a mandate to mimic physical reality. Why? This thesis is little more than a variation of Leibnitz's Doctrine of Pre-Established Har-

2. James, *Principles Psychology,* 141–47.

3. Clifford, *Body and Mind.*

4. Chalmers, *Conscious Mind.*

5. Hofstadter and Dennett, *The Mind's I*; Dennett and Kinsbourne, *Time Observer,* 183–247; Dennett, *Consciousness,* 433–35.

mony. Consciousness with these idle properties is highly unlikely and entirely pointless.

The second idea (numbered above) is that consciousness had an effect on the direction of evolution. If that were not so, then evolution would have no way to select against *inappropriate* conscious experiences. Consciousness might then have evolved in a way that diverged away from the direction taken by physiology. So a body that is currently engaged in making dinner might possess a psyche that is swimming the English Channel; and a body that is leading in a master's tournament might be subjectively sound asleep. *Why would it matter?* If consciousness doesn't matter, then why would its contents matter? *If it doesn't matter than it shouldn't matter what it is.*

It is concluded here that consciousness *does* matter. It produces a decisive causal influence, or force, that is not derivable from currently known physical forces. Physics does not now list consciousness as being the source of a separate force and has never seriously considered that possibility. This neglect is understandable because the supposed influence emerges in the most complicated physical system that the universe has yet produced—the conscious living organism. For that reason it would be difficult to untangle the influence of consciousness from other influences in order to document its presence and its properties. Most scientists therefore rest on the assumption that there is no such influence, inasmuch as they cannot *explain* that influence. Of course, they can't explain the influence of biology on consciousness either. Consciousness cannot be currently explained as cause or effect. It lies entirely outside of the current paradigm of physics. Nonetheless, almost everyone believes that physiology influences consciousness without understanding why. It is claimed here that the influence of consciousness on physiology is just as believable, although we don't understand that either. When we finally do crack the consciousness-biology code we will find that it is a two-way street like everything else in nature. To say that consciousness is caused without itself having effect is as puzzling as saying that it has effect without being caused. I therefore say it is both cause and effect—like everything else.

THE PARALLEL PRINCIPLE

The parallel principle states that:

> *Physiology and psychology evolve together in any conscious species, where each guides the evolution of the other onto parallel tracks.*

John von Neumann calls this a psychophysical parallelism.[6] It requires some degree of mutual monitoring between the two worlds to keep them together on parallel tracks. It means that objectivity and subjectivity must feed information to one another, completing the cycle of influence so the two can evolve together in a complementary way. If there were no feedback, there would be no way for evolution to select *against* a species that mutates in the direction of inappropriate (i.e., nonparallel) conscious experiences.

A GENERAL SUPPOSITION

An automaton operates on the basis of a simple stimulus-response sequence that is the sole variable in its evolutionary struggle. Suppose, as a result of mutation, a sequence appears in the form *stimulus-consciousness-response*. The conscious experience in this sequence does not have to be the sole determinant of the response, but we will allow that it is influential, that is, it will increase or decrease the likelihood of the response[7]. Specifically we will say that there are supportive experiences, such as pleasure or desire, that *always enhance* a response, and there are non-supportive experiences, such as pain or fear, that *always repress* a response. If the response favored by the newly introduced consciousness is wrong

---

6. von Neumann, *Mathematical Foundations*, 35.

7. Instead of using a straightforward stimulus-response mechanism, it has been suggested that some biological processes like photosynthesis and DNA mutations might proceed by choosing between competing quantum superpositions [Merali, *Quantum Life*, 44–49]. If this were the case then consciousness would not make a straightforward choice; but rather, it would influence probability distributions.

(i.e., if it enhances an unfortunate response), then the species will be less likely to survive. However, if the response is right, then the species will be more likely to survive. In the end, a successful species will have a conscious experience that is supportive and reflective of a successful stimulus-consciousness-response sequence, and that is the signature of a psychophysical parallelism.

The next section discusses *pain* experiences and how these might have been instrumental in establishing the parallel principle in a hypothetical primitive fish. In another place it is shown how other elementary motivational experiences (e.g., pleasure, fear, desire, love, anger, and so on) may have come into the evolutionary picture.[8]

A FANCIFUL FISH

Imagine an ancient fish that brushes against the toxic tentacles of a jellyfish. Assume that the fish has first learned to avoid the jellyfish tentacles *without* the help of consciousness, so it already has a nociceptive nervous system that favors withdrawal from their toxic contact. Otherwise, it would not have survived as long as it has. The nervous system of a fish is very primitive compared with humans, for it is dominated by brainstem components that lack a neocortex. In fact, the removal of the cerebral hemispheres of a fish does not inhibit its responses to noxious stimuli.[9] It is therefore easy to believe that fish are very robot-like creatures despite their frequent humanlike responses, and that they are a long way from a conscious evolutionary development. A fish is nonetheless chosen to illustrate the possible starting point of consciousness for reasons that are more picturesque than substantive.

Preconscious contact with the toxic tentacles will lead to two possible responses of the fish, that are labeled *CC* or *W* (continued contact or withdrawal). This is written

$$\text{contact leads to } +CC \text{ or } ++W \qquad (1)$$

8. Mould, *Evolution II*, 87–89; Mould, *Evolved Consciousness*, 141–45.

9. Rose, *Nature of Fish*, 1–38.

where $+CC$ represents the likelihood that the fish remains in "continued contact" with the tentacles, and $++W$ represents the likelihood that it "withdraws" from contact. The plus signs indicate the strength of the influence, so the double-plus sign in front of W means that the withdrawal response is more likely than continued contact. The preconscious fish has apparently evolved sufficiently to prefer W to CC, so it would be more likely to withdraw from the tentacles—hence its survival to date.

As the not-yet-conscious fish continues to evolve, mutations may occur that strengthen the withdrawal response, giving

$$\text{contact leads to } +CC +++W \qquad (2)$$

so W becomes even more probable than CC. After a number of mutations of this kind, the CC response will essentially disappear, leaving W as the only likely response. If the mutations mistakenly cause an increase in the probability of CC instead of W, then the species will probably not survive. Evolution will weed it out.

When pain consciousness is introduced the question becomes, "How will pain advance the evolution of this fanciful fish?" To satisfy the parallel principle, the pain associated with the contact state is *repressive* and this makes W much more probable, so statement #2 will be replaced by

$$\text{contact resulting in pain leads to } +CC ++++W \qquad (3)$$

Our assumption throughout is that the experience of pain will *always repress* the probability of the state that gave rise to it (in this case, CC), and/or it will *always support* the probability of the opposite state.

The difference between statements 1 and 2 is that a mechanical mutation has increased the likelihood of W; whereas in statement 3 another kind of mutation introduces pain into the contact state, and that increases the likelihood of W by an even greater amount. The first mutation in statement 2 appears to be more direct, and on that basis it might seem to be preferred. However, at some point the introduction of consciousness must have been the more favored route to survival. So statement 3 must have been preferred for reasons that are not clear at this time. Maybe consciousness is more efficient, allowing it to skip over +++W and go directly to ++++W or higher. Maybe a mutation that introduces a conscious experience is more easily achieved than one that tinkers with the nociceptive system alone. The answer to this will probably not be known until we understand how neurological networks introduce consciousness, and how that change might further affect the subject's response. But whatever the reason for this novel innovation, we can be sure that at some point statement 3 became the preferred path for some species; for it produced many species including our own in which pain is a vital subjective motivator that is well connected with the surrounding world, and that supports creature survival.

Pain in this example does not necessarily refer to the painful experience known to humans. Different creatures might experience pain differently.[10] What is important about pain is its repressive nature. Fear is also repressive, but in different ways in different physilogical situations.

ANCHOR FORCES

The universe appearing in the figure 2 of chapter 3 does not include anchor forces. The subjective universe in that diagram plays a causal role by being reflected in the subjective world. However, if subjectivity is to have a physical effect through anchor forces, we must indicate where those forces appear and where they go. We assume that the subjective universe is the theoretical origin of anchor forces, analogous to the way that the four forces of contemporary physics have their origin in the objective universe.

This anchor influence is shown in figure 3 in the form of a vertical tailed arrow that goes from the subjective universe to the objective universe, and a horizontal tailed arrow in the top row that goes from the objective universe to the objective world; plus

10. Nagel, *What's it Like,* 435–450.

a horizontal tailed arrow in the bottom row that goes from the subjective universe to the subjective world. So an anchor force originating in the subjective universe has a direct effect on the objective universe that in turn is a quantitative percept in the objective world, as well as a qualitative percept in the subjective world[11]. The remaining arrows in figure 3 are the same as those in figure 2.

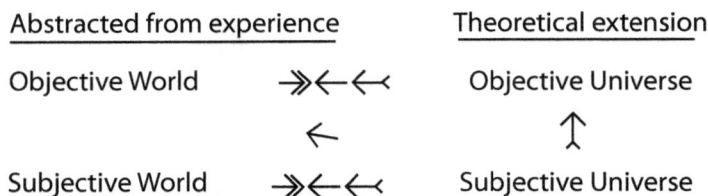

Abstracted from experience		Theoretical extension
Objective World	→»←←‹	Objective Universe
	←	↑
Subjective World	→»←←‹	Subjective Universe

Figure 3: Four parts of the universe including anchor forces

When the fanciful fish engages the toxic tentacles of the jellyfish, the encounter gives rise to a pain—represented by the tailed arrow in the bottom row. However, this pain will have no effect on the fish's evolution if the objective universe were not also affected in some way. The vertical tailed arrow represents that effect on the objective universe of the fish (i.e., on its brain), and it passes that effect along to the objective world of the fish. The fish's objective and subjective worlds are both modified when the fish breaks contact with the jellyfish's tentacles, and experiences relief.

CAUSE AND CHOICE

Statement 3 also allows the possibility of continued contact, which may be an alternative when the pain is not too overwhelming. In a sophisticated organism, *CC* may be accompanied by other conscious experiences that we might recognize as conflicting motivations, as in the case of an ascetic who makes a point of enduring

11. The subjective force (the tailed arrow on the bottom row of figure 3) might better be called a "subjective influence." It is nonetheless called a "force" to make it consistent with the use of the word in physics—referring to the effect of an interaction.

pain. The subject's subjective experience would then confirm that a *conscious choice* has been made between continued contact and withdrawal. That is, if two conscious motivations provide simultaneous stimuli in different directions, then, the subjective choice will be a conscious one.

However, that choice in the objective world is among causally determined probability amplitudes, and there is no reason to believe it is independent of those probabilities. There is no reason to believe that the choice is objectively "free," although that may be true within the subjective world. What the asthetic does in his experienced world is simply what he does. The conflict comes about in how he "explains" what he does, assuming that he is inclined to explanations.

5

MORALITY

A PURELY OBJECTIVE ACCOUNT of human experiences places us in an amoral world. The objective universe of science is (by itself) without moral imperatives; so moral behavior must involve subjective free-will to some extent. It involves a *fusion* of both the objective world and the subjective world. We humans are able to choose between right and wrong, where "right" and "wrong" are defined in terms of both subjective motivation as well as objective acting out.

There are two major categories of immorality: *Doing harm with malicious intent, and deriving satisfaction from doing harm to others.* Neither thoughts alone nor actions alone are immoral.

It is common to think that morality can be given an objective definition. This is simply not true. It is wrong to say that a mutually agreed upon crime such as stealing, or arson, or murder is itself immoral. Without taking the subjective component into account, these actions are merely parts of the objective world like a hurricane or a supernova that cannot be morally judged.

Morality is also thought to have a purely subjective significance. It is part of our religious tradition to impugn the morality of individuals who have evil thoughts, even though they don't act on those thoughts. I don't think so. I have evil thoughts that I do not pursue, and I do not go through my life feeling guilty about them. I also have positive thoughts, and I prefer to emphasize their importance in my life. The reason for this preference is apparent in the discussion of part II.

Morality cannot be given an absolute definition because it involves human judgment. It is an important judgment and important to realize that it has a dual disposition: objective and subjective; so our moral judgments are like our empirical observations in that they have a dual composition. This dualism is as essential to our notion of morality as it is to our notion reality. In both cases the raw experience is monistic.

It follows that preconscious creatures are neither moral nor immoral. Also, conscious creatures that do not exercise free-will for whatever reason are equally amoral because they fall outside of the above subjective categories. This chapter is an enumeration of examples that illustrate these points. Also in this chapter we look for ways to deal with a hostile world without ourselves becoming immoral. The notion of a good soldier is introduced as one who fights the good fight without moral recrimination. He is thereby spared pointless emotional distraction. The good soldier is complemented by the good juror who is required to judge the intensions of others on the basis of presented evidence, and who nonetheless realizes that an absolute knowledge of another's intentions is impossible.

As in chapter 3 we now include the *full* subjective world of the conscious individual that covers memories, instincts, and ideas, as well as sensations, feelings, and emotions. This fullness is essential if we are to make moral judgments.

JUDGING OTHERS

Adolf Eichmann was a SS lieutenant Colonel in Hitler's Third Reich. He was responsible for transporting thousands of Jews, gypsies, communists, homosexuals, and other "undesirables" to Nazi death camps during World War II. Toward the end of the war when it became clear that Germany would not win, Heinrich

Himmler (head of the SS) opened secret negotiations with the Allies, and in that connection he ordered Eichmann to stop sending railroad cars of new victims to the camps. But Eichmann continued to do so, ignoring Himmler's orders. Why did he do that?

At his trial in Jerusalem in 1961, Eichmann said that he was only doing his duty. He opposed Himmler briefly because Himmler was disregarding the law and ultimately the will of der Fuhrer. Eichmann's distracters accused him of malicious intent and of personal gratification in the demise of all these people. This would be second person subjective projection on their part and maybe they were right, but there is no way to know. It might be that Adolf Eichmann was only doing his duty as he said. What a strange fellow he would be—an automaton of sorts. But it is possible, and in that case he would be free of moral responsibility. Objectively, this murderous behavior was not immoral, however horrible it may seem to you, for *nothing* is objectively immoral. The abstract question, "Was Eichmann's behavior moral or immoral?" is meaningless because it pretends to be objective; whereas, his morality has much to do with how he regards his behavior.

A bombardier flying over Berlin in WWII would also have been an agent of mass killing. His bombs fell indiscriminately on hundreds of civilian women and children, some of whom were as innocent as his own wife and children. What was his motivation? He was probably possessed at that time by raw fear, and he probably just wanted to get his bombs away as soon as possible and head back to England. In moments of high stress people do not dwell on motives, so it is believable that he was just doing his duty as he would no doubt have said at the time. But emotions cannot be suppressed forever. What did he think when he gave the matter some thought? Where his emotions malicious, founded possibly on the danger he felt to himself and the harm done to his buddies or his country? Did he go so far as to feel a gleeful satisfaction when he had scored so boldly, raining down so much death and destruction? If so, then he was morally wrong whatever his claimed justification. Of course it is also possible that his motivations were never more than just doing an unpleasant job that had to be done.

He may have mentally "dehumanized" or "objectified" the people below him. It's possible that he and Eichmann were doing their duties like good soldiers, in which case they were both innocent. A good soldier does not kill maliciously or derive joy in doing so.

Both Eichmann and the bombardier may have qualified as good soldiers but it is not likely that they sustained that neutrality for very long or very consistently. It's likely that they both harbored resentments toward their victims who they believe to be members of a despicable race or creed, or who were allied with an incorrigible enemy. Humans do that sort of thing. It is hard to kill so many people without feeling guilt, and it is easy to blame the victim in order to acquit that guilt.

I was in the American Air Corps and was scheduled to go to flight training when the war in Germany ended in 1945. They told me they didn't need any more flight crew and that I had a choice between being assigned to a ground crew or accepting a discharge. I took the discharges and joined the Navy. Then in August following my boot leave the war in Japan was suddenly over. I was disappointed because I really wanted to kill somebody. Maybe I just wanted to be a war hero and kiss the girls. In any case, I would have gleefully taken the place of the bombardier, or so I thought at the time. I am sure that if I were in that position I would have been as petrified as anyone else. I am also sure that my thoughts on the subject would have been less than glorious. I don't think I actually hated anyone in the flesh, but I felt a general animus toward the people of the Third Reich and the Empire of the Rising Sun. When we dropped the atom bomb on Hiroshima I was jubilant. It was like we scored a fantastic touchdown.

I now see how these emotions connect to immorality—had I carried them out. I don't think it was malice on my part, but rather it was the second category of immorality. I would have felt a satisfaction in the demise of an enemy at my hand. I would have felt a patriotic pride in the destruction of another human being. War does that to people. It kills and wounds a great many, and it causes many to become immoral—not only for what they do, but because of what they think about what they do.

A private equity firm called PE took over a struggling manufacturing company called GAR that made gardening equipment ranging from hedge clippers to mowing machines. The company signed an agreement that gave PE wide control of its resources and facilities in the hope that bankruptcy might be avoided with new management that specialized in rescue operations of this kind. PE sold off some of those assets and reduced the work force to some extent. The effort seemed to work for a time, justifying the harsh treatment given to some of the employees. But it became increasingly clear that the plan would not work, at which point PE seemed to reverse direction. The firm drove the company further into debt and began appropriating its liquid assets. More of these assets were sold and more employees were let go. But this time the firm confiscated the pension and health benefits that the company had set aside for the employees. So the firm walked away with a huge profit, leaving the company's former employers and its debtors holding the bag, proving once again (to those who believe) that greed is good.

The strange thing is that firm's management saw no evil, or so they said. It is hard to imagine what the CEO and his fellow managers might have told themselves. On the face of it they were virtuous and successful entrepreneurs. They didn't violate the law so they claimed that nothing was wrong. Nothing? Employees who put thirty or more years into a company that provided for their pension and retirement health benefits were told that they were out on the street with nothing to show for it, and that the money would go instead to "bonuses for all" at PE. This is not to mention the merchants who extended credit in good faith to a firm that, toward the end, was dealing with them in bad faith. The firm obviously failed to do its intended job. That is not in itself wrong because success might have never been in the cards, and in any case the original intent was apparently good. But that intent turned sour. PE profited by the failure, and did so at the expense of many innocent souls.

Of course it is always possible that the CEO was just doing his job like a good soldier. It is certainly true that he got a big bonus when it was all over and so he profited from doing harm to others. But maybe he was oblivious to all of that like the bombardier whose only thought was to get his bombs away and return home. Maybe the CEO was only focused on maximizing the profits of PE as the stockholders tasked him to do, and in that case, his behavior was morally neutral. He was only doing his job.

However, so narrow a focus cannot be sustained forever. Emotions cannot be suppressed indefinitely. The question is: What did the CEO think about his behavior when he had a chance to think about it? It is hard for a person raised in a modern religion to do so much harm without feeling guilt. The CEO may not have taken many lives as did the bombardier and Adolf Eichmann, but he took many livelihoods and many well-earned retirements, and that can be just as devastating. It can cause as much long-term hurt to the living. So in order to combat guilt the CEO did the human thing. He demonized his victims. He tells the world that he was just doing his duty, and he tells himself that they had it coming. He tells himself that they were underachievers: takers and not makers. He regards his victims with contempt because they live off the achievements of others. With language like that his motives become malicious, and he allows himself to relish his victory. He thereby lines up both categories of immoral behavior against himself.

Question: How can it be said that people who do really evil things aren't evil? **Answer**: The question pretends to be objective. The universe of science makes no statement of this kind—one way or another. If good and evil are to be defined at all, then there must be a good or evil subjective component in the mind of the agent who performs the act.

HURRICANES

If a hurricane hits your town you defend yourself against it as best you can. You move lawn furniture into the basement and barricade the windows. However, you do not accuse the hurricane of an immoral act. That's because the objective world that includes the hurricane is incapable of immorality.

You should also defend yourself against the likes of Adolf Eichmann and the CEO of PE by fighting back in whatever way you can—the equivalent of moving the lawn furniture and barricading the windows. You might also accuse them of immorality because you know that they are capable of that. However, it is equally possible to think of Eichmann and the CEO as part of the objective world like a hurricane, and to that extent it is senseless to accuse them of immorality. Objectively speaking Eichmann, the CEO, and the hurricane are all amoral. They each represent the working out of the natural order of things. Of course Eichmann and the CEO have subjective lives unlike the hurricane; but since you have no knowledge of their subjectivity, you are better served by withholding disapproval and concentrating on defending yourself against them as you would a hurricane. In the interest of your own sanity and clear-headedness, you are best served by treating the enemy as an amoral force in nature that must be defended against and defeated in the best possible way. That's what a good soldier would do. Moral condemnation of the aggressor is a waste of time and energy leading primarily to ulcers. It's best to focus on behavior. We don't really know what is going on in another person's mind, so we don't really know if he is immoral or not.

The good soldier has emotions of course, but they can be taught to be positive—to regret rather than relish the harm done to others. This suggests that the good soldier might lack the motivation to put up a good fight. However, he might very well have the passion to drive his case home because of his conviction, dedication, and loyalty to those he defends. His feelings need not include vengeance, maliciousness, or satisfaction in seeing harm done to others. The latter emotions cloud thinking, whereas the former are more effective when dealing with hurricanes or humans. Unfortunately, most humans don't work that way.[1]

1. Contrast the conflicting attitudes of Generals George Patton and Omar Bradley during World War II. Patton went into battle joyfully; whereas Bradley

REWARD AND PUNISHMENT

The above understanding of morality does not provide reward and punishment in the usual religious sense. There is no judgment in the afterlife because there is no afterlife. Instead, moral consequences are to be found in the writings of humanists and to some extent the claims of eastern philosophers. If an individual wants to live in a society of decent people then he must present that example to the world. He must teach his children by word and by example to follow the golden rule. Humans are naturally empathetic to one another, and this sympathy must be cultivated if we are to realize the benefits of a civilized society.

The Law of Karma says, in the current vernacular, "what goes around comes around." Those who live a violent life will reap violence in the end. Those who deceive will attract deceivers to themselves, and those who exploit others are game for exploitation. Also, one who is honest and virtuous in his dealings will attract the trust and loyalty of others who are themselves honest and virtuous in their dealings. These ideas: violence, deceit, exploitation, trust, and virtue have no objective meaning, so they only have a subjective significance. The Law of Karma appears to be a subjective directive.

The subjective universe contains all moral and immoral experiences, and gets hit from both ends of a moral or immoral transaction. It not only experiences an instance of harmful intent, but at the same time, it experiences the harm that results from that intent. For the subjective universe the Law of Karma says: what goes around *is* around. In chapter 11 we will see how an individual's karma is affected by this connection to the subjective universe.

---

remained cool, deliberate, and very effective. As a counterpoint to the above thesis, Patton was also very effective. Perhaps his driving force was a joy of combat more than hating the enemy.

THE LAW

Right and wrong as prescribed by the law are part of the objective world. They are a codification of behavior that tries to avoid subjective language as much as possible. We humans establish these laws in the hope that they will provide security for our lives and property. The laws are not themselves moral or immoral, for nothing in the objective world can be right or wrong in that way. The law may mention a person's "motive" or "intension," but it speaks of these things as though they were measurable quantities Expert witnesses testify on these matters, but they are portrayed in court as scientists reporting objective fact. The law pretends objectivity in order to protect our objective selves from the harmful acts of others, and once put to paper, we preach that they should be obeyed as though they were objective laws of nature.

We have seen that the definition of morality includes subjective states of mind, so any attempt to objectify or codify morality is bound to be inadequate. Consider the King James Commandment "Thou shalt not kill." Because there are many forms of killing that are state approved such as (a) in self-defense, (b) in time of war, (c) in the execution of felons, (d) in the abortion of a fetus, and (e) in stepping on cock roaches and other nasties, the commandment seems to be a poor statement of what is intended. The Jewish and English Standard versions "You shall not murder" or simply "Do not murder" seem more to the point. However, there is a catch. How do you define murder? There are those who say that the execution of felons is not murder, but that the abortion of a fetus is murder. There are those who say that wartime killing is state sponsored murder, and still others wag a finger at the slaughter of animals for human consumption. Murder is a derogatory term that cannot be objectively defined. Killing can be objectively defined. It means destroying life and that is clear enough. But murder is a subjective term that means *an unacceptable way of killing*. If you disapprove of executing felons you call it murder. If you disapprove of abortion you call it murder. When you use the pejorative term "murder" to describe any form of killing you are merely expressing your strong disapproval of that form of killing.

So how do we state the commandment without having to make endless exceptions and without using subjective terminology? It's not easy. A person charged with murder defends himself before a judge and jury. Both the prosecution and the defense argue the law. If that were all that mattered then guilt or innocence would be established on objective grounds only, independent of subjectively defined morality or immorality. However, the final verdict is placed in the hands of a jury. The jury is instructed in the law during the trial but they are not legal professionals. They are better qualified to make subjective judgments about states of mind such as motive. In the end, it is the jury that decides the case. Even if there is overwhelming evidence of a crime, and the accused admits the crime, and by any reading of the law the accused is guilty of the crime, the jury is still empowered to declare the accused innocent if it is so inclined. That's because right or wrong (or good or evil) involves subjective judgments that are rooted in one or more of the two categories of immoral behavior. A defendant is on trial for days or weeks in the company of two or more professional lawyers and a prestigious judge. All that judicial firepower and the final decision is placed in the hands of amateurs. This tells us how much we depend on objective measures, and how much we distrust them to give the right answer.

THE GREAT IRONIST

Socrates ridiculed Athenian politicians and noblemen because they said and did things based solely on their instincts. They rarely bothered to give reasons for those instincts, and when they did attempt to explain themselves they usually came up with an unconvincing rationalization. Nietzsche claims that Socrates began to (secretly) laugh at himself for much the same reason. I have no idea how Nietzsche came to know such a thing, but he says that Socrates began to suspect that he too relied on his instincts in a way that could not be accounted for rationally. Socrates was said to argue with himself "But why must we free ourselves of our instincts? We have to help both them *and* reason, come into their own—we have to follow our instincts, but convince our reason to lend them a helping hand with good arguments." Nietzsche here attributes Socrates with a modern idea. He says that instinct and reason are equal partners that work hand in glove with one another. Nietzsche continues: "This was the real *duplicity* of the great ironist, so full of secrets; he induced his conscience to content itself with a sort of self-deception; at bottom he grasped the irrational aspect of moral judgments."[2]

It is not really correct to say that moral judgments are intrinsically irrational, for they can be either rational or irrational. They are simply judgments that are found within the subjective worldview, and rationality is something that can be applied to either world. We can reason about things in the objective world and/ or about things in the subjective world.

We argue in today's secular world about the hereditary or environmental origin of instincts, but most of us do not debate their legitimacy. Not so in Nietzsche's day. Throughout his lifetime "instincts" were widely assumed to be a base residue of original sin. His contemporaries would not have understood the idea that instincts could stand morally toe to toe with reason. But instinct is a part of the subjective world and reason is a way of thinking about either world. Neither instinct nor reason is intrinsically moral or immoral, nor is the domain of one reducible to the domain of the other.

THREADING THE NEEDLE

The legal expectation is that a jury will apply reason to the evidence presented in court and do the reasonable thing. Juries generally try to do that. Or at least, that's their understanding of what they're supposed to do. But reason cuts both ways. It applies to the intuitions of the individual jurist as well as to the articulated law.

2. Nietzsche, *Good and Evil*, 79.

Everyone in the jury box has instincts about what is right and what is wrong concerning what is presented in court; and in the end it is mostly instinct that prevails. A good lawyer knows that and he knows that he is not supposed to know that. In principle he argues an objectively given law before a jury of empty vessels. In practice, he does his best to read their minds and bend his case accordingly. Our legal system attempts to thread the needle between objectivity and subjectivity, which is probably an impossible thing to do once those gestalts are in place. We want standards of public morality that are strictly enforced, and we know instinctively that there is no such thing. The best we can do is come together on what the law should be and how it should be applied, and leave it to a handful of citizens to settle disputes. It is their job to reason about the law and their own instincts, and to stitch the two together.

GOOD SOLDIER AND GOOD JUROR

The good soldier is said to withhold moral judgment about his foe. He treats the enemy like a hurricane—like a force of nature that must be dealt with objectively without unsavory negative passions. He doesn't know what is going on in the mind of his battlefield opponent, so he does his duty without himself become immoral by killing maliciously or deriving joy in doing so. He reaps the benefit of clarity of mind and purpose, working together with positive motivations.

Of course, it may be useful to know as much as possible about an opponent's state of mind as it pertains to intent, especially as it pertains to "immoral" intent. Maybe you cannot know what he is thinking, but you can make intelligent guesses. For that purpose, the model is a "good juror."

The good juror is one who carefully views the evidence and listens to the arguments while sitting in dispassionate judgment. He evaluates rational connections. Of course this much can be done by the good soldier. However, the good juror adds his own unique contribution when he makes subjective evaluations to determine moral culpability. He knows that he cannot know what is going on in the mind of another, but he can draw on his knowledge of himself. He can connect with his own instincts and imagine what it must be like to pervert those instincts as argument suggests. He can recognize base motives that he finds in himself, and project their destructive employment onto another. He puts purely subjective impressions together with the objective picture that is being drawn, and finds rational compatibility. If on that basis a moral or immoral motivation is plausible, then the verdict is all the more believable. There is a legal tradition that says that if you cannot find a motive then guilt is questionable. That is probably a good rule for each of us to follow when we call on our own good juror to judge the morality of another.

When the good juror finds a verdict his job is done. The case then reverts to the good soldier who again deals with the hurricane.

Question: Is a person immoral if he derives satisfaction from someone else doing harm to another? **Answer**: No! However, it is unhealthy for him to entertain negative feeling of this kind for reasons given in chapter 11. These sentiments can harm him if he dwells on them, but he is not himself immoral if he does not act on them.

6

SECOND CAUSE

—————

IN THIS CHAPTER WE investigate *nonanchor experiences* that includes data coming into awareness through sight, sound, and other information gathering sensations concerning the external world. These experiences have an influence that takes the form of identifying and bringing forth gestalts that have a degree of intelligibility that only consciousness can provide. They express their influence in the objective world through "nonanchor" forces.

In the case of vision, the brain receives an image from the eyes that goes first to the visual cortex, and from there it is broken up and transmitted to various parts of the cerebral cortex. The brain then manages to take this widely distributed raw data and form it into a recognizable image that has a distinct location in space. The brain therefore *forms a gestalt* at the level of ordinary observation—it organizes the scattered visual information in an understandable way. It is argued in this chapter that for conscious creatures, consciousness plays an important role in the selection of novel observational gestalts. It is this influence of consciousness that is carried out at the objective level by nonanchor forces.

ANCHOR REVIEW

We have already introduced *anchor experiences* that include feelings or emotions such as pleasure, pain, anger, fear, and love. Anchor-based forces repress or enhance experiences like the painful experience of the fanciful fish in chapter 4, and they produce a species that satisfies the parallel principle by bringing mind and body together. These forces are not yet documented by physics, but it is our claim that they must exist because there is no other way to explain the psychophysical parallelism of von Neumann. Sensations like touch, taste, and smell perform both nonanchor and anchor functions at different times .[1]

NONANCHOR GESTALTS

Experiences such as sight and sound are accompanied by *nonanchor forces* that have a far less obvious influence than do anchor forces. To understand their effect it is necessary to comprehend how the brain goes about the construction of an image on the basis of information coming to it by way of something like sight. First, a note on what does not happen. It is safe to say that signals coming into the eye and moving along the optic nerve into the brain *do not* finally project an image on a neurological screen—like a moving picture.[2] Instead, bits and pieces of the information streaming along the optic nerve are sent first to the visual cortex, and from there they spread out to higher areas of the brain. A single object of perception like a "pencil" is broken up according to color and shape and transmitted to different parts of the higher cortex. The "paper clip" lying next to the pencil is also disassembled according to color and shape and sent to *other* parts of the higher cortex. The question is then: How do the separated parts of either one of these objects manage to get reassembled into a single object of perception? This is called the *binding problem* and it is a major problem

---

1. Mould, *Evolution II,* 87–89; Mould, *Evolved Consciousness,* 141–45.
2. Crick and Koch, *Theory of Consciousness,* 263–75.

in brain functioning. There are conflicting accounts concerning how this works.[3]

There is another problem. Even if all the parts of the pencil are reassembled into a single object of perception (as distinguished from the parts of the paper clip that are reassembled into another percept) there remains the question of how the bits and pieces of the pencil are reassembled into a recognizable pencil rather that a mish-mash of colors and shapes. This is called the *recognition problem* and is also a current problem in brain functioning. It is the temporal lobe of the brain that organizes the assembled information of an object into a recognizable form. We know this because brain damage in parts of this area can impair a person's ability to recognize things.[4] For instance, brain psychologists are able to locate "face recognition" capability at a specific location in the temporal lobe.

Persons with brain damage in this area can see faces but they do not recognize them. They may not even recognize their own face in a mirror. Evidently the brain first forms a *binding gestalt* that assembles a face-object, as opposed to a leg-object or a typewriter-object. It then recognizes the face if that area in the temporal lobe is functioning properly. So the normally seen face is the result of a two-part gestalt: A binding part and a recognition part. Theories abound, but we do not know how the brain does these things.

And finally there is the matter of location in space. Simply because images fall on the retina in a spatially ordered way, giving one location to the pencil and another location to the paper clip, does not mean that the final cortical destination of the bits and pieces of both these objects will preserve the original retinal positions, and it does not. Otherwise there would be a neurological screen on which these objects are projected, and there is no evidence for that. So the question is: How is it that these two objects

---

3. Chalmers, *Character of Consciousness*; Crick and Koch, *Theory of Consciousness*, 263–75; Dennett and Kinsbourne, *Time Observer*, 183–247; Engel et al., *Temporal Binding*, 128–51; O'Regan and Noë, *Account Vision*, 939–1031; O'Regan, *Red Doesn't Sound Like*; Singer, *Consciousness-Binding*, 123–146

4. Carlson, *Physiology*.

get recognizably reassembled in two different ways that reflect their different positions in the external space of the observer? This is the *location problem*. It is the parietal lobe of the brain that assigns final visual locations to each object. Brain damage in parts of this area can disable this capability.

We now have three reassembly problems: (1) Binding the bits and pieces of perception together in such a way that each object gathers into a separate figure that is distinct from other objects. (2) Assembling each figure so that it is recognized for what it is supposed to be. (3) Locating each figure in a spatial relationship (i.e., figure/ground) that reflects its position in the external world. All three of these assemblies are current problems in brain functioning. There is much speculation as to how this is done.

Nonetheless, the brain somehow manages to pull together these diverse bits and pieces of information and organize them into an intelligible and recognizable picture of the external world. *The brain completes a gestalt* using data scattered over the cortex.

COMPLEXITY

Complex systems of many variables have a way of generating internal patterns of those variables. These patterns are the subject of "complexity theory."[5] Presumably the brain is a complex system of neurons that produce patterns of a kind described by the theory, and it is reasonable to suppose that this is the source of the above gestalts.[6] We will therefore assume that complexity theory describes the underlying *physical mechanism* that gives rise to organized brain patterns, or gestalts. However, that theory alone cannot determine which of these patterns is brought forward as a conscious gestalt. Something outside of complexity theory must make choices of that kind.

For a non-conscious organism, the choice among competing complexity-theory brain patterns is governed by heredity and/

5. Heylighen *Comlexity*; Donderi *Visual Complexity* 73–97
6. Bob, *Brain and Mind,* 17–22.

or by environmental influences, and it is strictly deterministic. The gestalt is mechanically chosen on the basis of robotic forces, although of course the gestalt is not "experienced." However, for a conscious being there is a requirement beyond those purely mechanical conditions. The chosen gestalt must also have a property of "intelligibility." An intelligible gestalt *might be* selected by heredity and/or environment factors alone—but not necessarily. When gestalts arise that are unfamiliar in a new and challenging world, it may be that only consciousness can provide the enabling intelligibility. It isn't clear why nature introduced consciousness into the universe in the first place. Maybe hard-wired robots do not have the flexibility to respond to novel situations. Maybe they cannot deal with astonishing new ideas, or have a world-shattering epiphany. It is therefore supposed that the gestalt that rises to the level of consciousness is *determined in part by consciousness itself.* Consciousness has a physical effect in that it participates in gestalt selection. It may also aid complexity theory by playing a part in the *formation* of a gestalt. We call the forces associated with either effect *nonanchor forces.*

The subjective universe in figure 4 is shown to be the source of the nonanchor influence. The subjective universe is not just the origin of all the subjective experiences plus anchor forces, it is the instigator of nonanchor forces as well. This influence is indicated in the diagram by the horizontal double-tailed arrow that goes from the subjective universe to the subjective world in the bottom row. Also, the vertical double-tailed arrow in the diagram above the subjective universe identifies a complementary influence on the objective universe that affects changes in the structure of the brain.

That change in brain structure goes together with a change in the perceived subjective world, but that may or may not result in a change in the objective world. The person *may not act* on the new gestalt, in which case the objective world is unchanged; or the person *may act* on the new gestalt, in which case the objective world of the individual is changed by the action performed. For this reason, the horizontal double-tailed arrow on the top row in figure 4 is accompanied by a question mark.

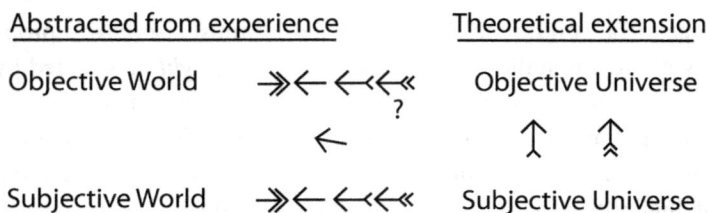

Abstracted from experience   Theoretical extension

Objective World   →← ←‹←«   Objective Universe
                            ?
              ←   ↑   ↑

Subjective World   →← ←‹←«   Subjective Universe

Figure 4: Four parts of the universe including nonanchor forces

Consider the case of a conscious creature that views the line drawing of the Other Woman appearing in the first chapter. Each segment in that line drawing is separately processed in the creature's primary visual cortex and that information is passed on to higher areas of its brain. However, there is no neurological projection screen in the brain that completely reproduces the external scene; nonetheless, the conscious brain somehow organizes this information (via complexity theory) into at least two gestalts—the young woman and the old woman. The one that is brought forward in experience is chosen by any number of factors including hereditary and environmental as well as its intelligibility. The latter may not play an exclusive role, or maybe none at all, but it does play a role in novel situations; and to that extent it engages nonanchor forces. Of course, there may be other complexity brain patterns in the mix that are not candidates for an experienced gestalt, because they fail the test of nature, nurture, or intelligibility.

The described influence is visual, but nonanchor forces are also associated with hearing. Other modes of sensations such as touch, smell, and taste can function as nonanchor influences as well as anchor influences.

When a conscious creature "flips" from one gestalt to another, intelligibility becomes a more important factor. There is no reason to believe that a non-conscious creature can switch gestalts at all, but conscious beings certainly can; and switching from an established gestalt to something new can introduce a novelty that goes beyond the reach of heredity or previous experience. In that case consciousness might be the dominant factor in the selection of a new gestalt.

Only consciousness can provide intelligibility in situations that are sufficiently novel that neither hereditary nor previous experience can fully account for the choice. The brain knows how to select new gestalts, and it is the claim of this book that *intelligibility plays a critical role in selecting new gestalts for subjective viewing, and in reinforcing established gestalts*. Nonanchor forces provide the necessary causal influence. They also carry through with an influence on the objective universe, and possibly on the objective world.

TIME-SPAN GESTALTS

Not only does an individual's brain organize bits and pieces that are in the brain at a given moment of time, but it can also include data that appears in the cortex of the brain at *different times*. It forms a four dimensional gestalt.[7]

If you were sitting in the front row of a movie theater, assuming that the speakers are up front with the screen, then the light from the screen and sound waves from the speakers would reach you at virtually the same time. You would therefore see the picture and hear the sound at the same time. However, someone sitting in the back row would receive the light waves and the sound waves at different times because light travels faster than sound. If a gun is fired in the movie, then the sight and the sound of the explosion would arrive at the front row simultaneously; but the sound waves would arrive at the back of the theater some time after the light waves. In that case you would expect someone sitting in the back to experience sensual dissonance. They would see and hear the shot at different times. That would be true *if* the difference in time between sight and sound is more than 80 milliseconds.

7. Eagleman, *Timing signals and perception*

However, if the person in the back row is close enough to the front so that the time difference is less than 80 ms, then he would experience the sight of the shot and the report of the shot *at the same time*, just like the person in the front row. How is that possible? Apparently the gestalt formed by the brain *provides for the simultaneity* of things that are *supposed to be simultaneous*. That's the meaning of intelligibility in this case. Even though the brain receives these stimuli at different times, it manages to form a gestalt that brings the two cortical events together so they are experienced together. Within the 80 ms range of time difference, everyone in the theater will see the flash of the gun at the same time they hear it go off, because brain gestalt formation stretches over space and time.

SUBJECTIVE DISCRETION

We assume that the subjective universe does not have a separate superbrain. It includes all the undifferentiated elements of consciousness that are not reflected by brains, plus all of the differentiated elements of consciousness that are reflected by brains, but it does not have a separate brain of its own to process information. However, because the subjective universe is the bearer of all conscious experiences including free-will, it is able to exercise some *discretion* in its limited role. Through its ambient free-will, the subjective universe extends its function by helping to chose *which gestalts* are brought forward for the individual.

The subjective universe cannot be arbitrary in that selection Its choice must be truly intelligible to the individual, but where there is some ambiguity on that point, the subjective universe is empowered to exert some direction. This does not require a separate brain. It means that the subjective universe has its own tendencies and inclinations, and it has an ability through free-will to influence the gestalt choices made by individuals.

Normally the subjective universe selects gestalts that are based on a creature's own locally determined preference. What is intelligible to me, with my prejudices and self-interests, will normally carry the day when it comes to my selection of gestalts. In that case, the subjective universe yields to my better judgment as to what is good for me. But the subjective universe is in a position to override me. Intelligibility influenced by self-interest has a cosmic dimension, and that may modify the role of consciousness in the selection of my gestalts. *The sum of all generated self-interest is not necessarily acceptable to the whole,* so we allow cosmic intelligibility to prevail where there is good reason. We give the subjective universe an ability to judge—to determine how it deploys nonanchor forces over all.

When selecting one of the women in the Other Woman gestalt we are generally satisfied to make that choice without partiality, since we are not likely to have a stake in the outcome. But when we choose from among social, political, economic or religious gestalts, it's another matter. Generally speaking we then have something to gain or to lose; so we place two requirements on our gestalts: They must be intelligible *and* they must promote our interests. They must fulfill some "purpose" of our own.

The same is true at the level of the total subjective universe. It not only has a selection ability from among potential individual gestalts, but it also has a stake in the outcome because it may have cosmic interests to be satisfied. What these interests are will be the subject of future chapters. For the moment we say only that: By making use of the intelligibility of consciousness, *the subjective universe encourages gestalts that serve wider interests.* The subjective universe is not only a depository and a source of creature consciousness, but it has willful discretion as well.

The subjective universe is therefore an independent judge of the direction of evolution. The claim is that the subjective universe not only fulfills our many expressions of self-interest, but it also serves the self-interest of the whole by preferentially upholding or restraining gestalts that are brought forward in individual experiences. It is through this influence that the subjective universe plots a course in history that is favorable to the well being of us all. Evidence will be presented in part II that supports this idea.

This mechanism clarifies the way in which the universe uses conscious creatures to address its interests, and how we humans have become the leading edge of that enterprise. We are uniquely qualified for this task. No doubt primitive conscious creatures act on the basis of gestalts, but we go much further. We base our civilizations on formative gestalts. We have social, political, economic, religious, and scientific gestalts that define our culture; and it is a culture that evolves from one civilization to the next in a relatively short period of time. We are therefore ideal beings in this part of the universe for carrying out the purpose of the subjective universe.

Question: If a choice that I make is determined by free-will rather than scientific determinism, then what is the source of free-will? How and where does it come from? **Answer**: Free-will is allocated to each conscious individual. The total free-will of the entire population is identical with cosmic free-will. Since most gestalt selections are domestic and robotic, few of our decisions are instances of free-will—but some are.

PART II

7

COSMIC PURPOSE

THE SUBJECTIVE UNIVERSE IS found to be independently willful and it impresses itself on the imaginations of the conscious creatures of the universe. Humans who look to meaning and purpose in their lives will readily attach themselves to something greater than themselves, and that can take the form of accepting cosmic direction.[1] This yearning we find in ourselves is promoted through nonanchor forces that act in the subjective worlds of all conscious creatures, but they are especially effective on intellectually flexible humans. It is through these forces that the subjective universe promotes gestalts in humans that are favorable to its purpose, and in doing so it places an enlightened finger on the scale of human history.

In this chapter, we examine one form that that purpose might take. Since the subjective universe experiences every instance of inflicted pain on conscious creatures, *it is in its own interest to minimize the pain and suffering throughout the universe, and at the same time to maximize pleasure.* There may be other forms of cosmic purpose, but we will focus on this humane candidate in the remaining chapters of the book. Cosmic purpose, I say in this

---

1. Kristof and WuDunn, *A Path Appears*; Gawande, *Being Mortal,* 123–27.

chapter, is to minimize pain and maximize pleasure through the introduction of facilitating gestalts.

DOMESTIC PURPOSE

If your purpose is the accumulation of wealth, then the purpose of the universe is for you to accumulate wealth. If your purpose is to enter the Olympics, then the purpose of the universe is for you to enter the Olympics; and if it is your purpose to give aid to a fallen kin, then the purpose of the universe is for you to aid a fallen kin. In this sense the subjective universe is full of domestic purposes that are expressed through the many conscious creatures in its domain. These purposes are standard fare. They are to be found in one form or another in every conscious species. They are the accumulated self-interests of individuals that will be called the *domestic purpose* of the subjective universe.

If the purpose of the universe refers only to the domestic purpose so defined, then the claim that the universe has a purpose is trivially true. But that is not the intent of a claim that goes above and beyond domestic purpose. That claim refers to an enlightened purpose that is superimposed on domestic purpose and realized through conscious creatures such as ourselves. The subjective universe supports *cosmic purpose*.

This conjecture is not an anthropomorphic projection. Cosmic purpose would be an anthropomorphism if it were projected onto the objective universe, but our definition of cosmic purpose only projects subjective qualities onto the subjective universe; so it is consistent with the nature of the projected domain. Compatibility is preserved.

A FINGER ON THE SCALE

The subjective universe has an autonomy of its own and it exercises free-will on its own. It furthermore does so on behalf of cosmic purpose. The subjective universe thereby uses free-will to favor those experiences that support its purpose. It accomplishes this by calling forth gestalts that fulfill its cosmic objectives in the manner described in chapter 6.

If the entire human race is content with its present social, political, economic, and religious institutions then cosmic purpose will not intervene, for in that case the subjective universe will be resigned to the status quo—fulfilling domestic purpose only. It will place a finger on the scale only when there is sufficient desire for change, and it will do so by bringing forward intelligible alternatives that might otherwise go unnoticed. This describes the familiar situation in which most people in a population are conservatively content with an established way of thinking, while a minority is looking for something different. Change occurs only when the desire of the minority gains sufficiency.

We creatures therefore set the stage for cosmic purpose and at the same time we are its surrogates. Free-will is a characteristic of the subjective universe that is vested in individuals, but we don't own it any more than we own anything else. Free-will "belongs" to the universe as a whole, manifesting itself at the level of the subjective universe and reflected by humans in the subjective world—whether it is a domestic or a cosmic variety.

THE PURPOSE OF PURPOSE

Recall that the subjective universe experiences all of the moral rights and wrongs of its inhabitants. It inflicts the benefit and harm done to all, and it simultaneously receives the benefit and harm done by all. I said previously that the Principle of Karma applied to the subjective universes is: "What goes around *is* around." The subjective universe experiences all the instances of good and bad that are passed along by one of us to another one of us, not to mention the benefit and harm done to us by natural forces. The life of conscious creatures has its ups and downs. It can be brutal because of the acts of others or because of acts of nature, and it can be joyous for either one of those reasons.

It is therefore assumed that *the subjective universe will want to minimize harm and maximize pleasure* inasmuch as it experiences both. But how can it do that? You have free-will and you want to minimize if not remove all of the harm done to yourself, as well as maximize the pleasure in your life, but you cannot do that unopposed because there are too many objective barriers and constraints as well as the reluctance of you and your fellow humans to change. There are similar limitations on the subjective universe. It may want to fine-tune the degree of benefit and harm done throughout the universe, but there are too many barriers and constraints. For instance, the universe was originally set up to run along lines that *use pain* as an evolutionary tool. Therefore, pain cannot be completely eliminated without destroying the mechanics of the entire system. It cannot be removed with the snap of a finger. The subjective universe must work with the evolutionary product at hand, and that has built-in tendencies to inflict pain on others.

So if the cosmic purpose of the subjective universe wants to manage its own joy and suffering, it cannot do so instantaneously. It must proceed more cautiously. It must use the causal influence of consciousness to ease the direction of evolution along the desired route. The subjective universe has a nonanchor force accessibility to the subjective and objective worlds to this end. This is indicated by the double-tailed arrow in the bottom row of figure 4 of chapter 6 and the complementary up arrow above the subjective universe in that diagram. This nonanchor influence can change the way an entire species understands its situation by bringing fourth revised gestalts, but it cannot proceed unopposed. It must find its way through a maze of obstacles and that takes time, so we look for a long-term historic influence.

Remember that the subjective universe does not have a brain of its own so it cannot engage in independent long range planning. It can only stumble onto things like the collection of conscious individuals within its fold. If it wants to supervise pleasure and pain it is as uncertain as the included individuals as to how to go about that. Using idealistic gestalts to deliver change is a slow and hazardous journey that is not likely to make a rapid difference in biological evolution, especially for low-level species.

However, the leading edge of that evolution in our part of the universe is the human race that is different from other species in some important ways. We rarely devour one another so we rarely inflict pain through predator/prey dealings; instead, we excel in doing harmful things to our fellow creatures *and* we show extraordinary kindness. In addition, we humans follow patterns of behavior that are highly dependent on social norms, so our way of doing harm and giving pleasure is very socially dependent. As a result, our concept-based culture is ideal for receiving direction from newly introduced gestalts. If the cosmic purpose of the universe is to reduce pain and intensify pleasure, then humans are ideal mechanisms of change.

We cannot be sure that cosmic purpose exists, much less know what it is. However, it is reasonable to believe that *the subjective universe will strive to minimize its suffering and maximize its satisfaction by encouraging more idealistic gestalts, and we humans will generally experience this encouragement over extended periods of time.* This is one formulation of cosmic purpose and we should look for evidence of that purpose in the history of human affairs. It need not be the *only* cosmic purpose. Reducing its own suffering and enhancing its satisfaction is at least one component of its purpose, but the mechanism is in place for other forms to be expressed. We will later consider more exotic candidates, but we will first examine the more modest possibility.

Maybe this account underestimates cosmic purpose and that the subjective universe is indeed capable of long range planning. Maybe it does have a sort of cosmic brain after all—one that envisions and executes universal purpose. Maybe it can form its own gestalts. Nonetheless, we will not go that far in this book. We will continue to assume that the subjective universe is just a sum of the undifferentiated elements of consciousness that have not been reflected by brains, plus the differentiated elements of consciousness that have been reflected by brains, so it can only stumble onto a successful strategy for the reduction of suffering. Consistent with that, and with its holistic overview and its free-will, the subjective universe very sensibly looks for ways to reduce the pain that it feels, and to maximizes its pleasure. This is the subjective universe's cosmic purpose, and on its behalf, the subjective universe places an enlightened finger on the scale of history. It should be possible to recognize that influence, so in the following chapter we will look for evidence. We will be looking for the *zeitgeist* of different periods of history that relate to the alleviation of human suffering.

8

THE EVIDENCE

————

WHAT IS THE EVIDENCE that the subjective universe strives to maximize human pleasure and minimize pain? It isn't long ago that Christians tortured those who were believed to stray from the faith, and it isn't long ago that the Roman public cheered as gladiators battled to death in the arena. Human propensity to violence has softened dramatically in the West since those times; and in fact, violence has decreased remarkably throughout the entire world going back to pre-biblical times. Steven Pinker has amassed extensive evidence to this effect.[1] We will not attempt to match that effort in this book, but we will survey two of the major Western liberating movements of recent centuries. First, there was the struggle for religious tolerance that in the twentieth century became the ecumenical movement. This sentiment was given a boost when the world became aware of the detestable treatment of the Jews during World War II. It is typical of every step forward that it is preceded by some horrible experience.

The rights movement is something quite separate with a history of its own. In America it began with the Bill of Right and took a historic turn a half-century later during a devastating civil war. We spend much of this chapter examining the various rights

1. Pinker, *Better Angles.*

movements that gained prominence in nineteenth and twentieth century America. This has resulted in some dramatic and sometimes surprising developments. However conservative the American public seems to be on so many fronts, most people have become amazingly tolerant of their fellow creatures. While this enumeration of hard won rights is not a proof of cosmic purpose, it lends itself to a belief that there is a steady progress toward more humane institutions, and that bodes well for cosmic purpose as formulated above.

RELIGIOUS TOLERANCE

There has been a dramatic increase of religious tolerance in the West over the past several centuries. Christian civilization was at war with itself in the fifteenth century in a conflict that lasted well into modern times. Overt conflict subsided by the eighteenth century, for by that time the doctrine of separation of church and state had found its way into enlightened thinking. But it wasn't until the middle of the twentieth century that the ecumenical principle was widely accepted in the West.

In World War II the armed forces of the United States recognized three chaplains: Protestant, Catholic, and Jewish, thereby giving formal recognition to Judaism as having an equal status with the Christianity. However, there remained an undertone of disapproval of Jews in America. Jews escaping Nazi Germany in the 1930s were refused entrance to U.S. ports, and it was common at that time for country clubs and other fraternities and societies to restrict membership by excluding Jews. Jews were cautiously accepted but with many hesitations. "He's a Jew" was often whispered.

It took a decade or so, but the Holocaust did have an effect on our thinking. Jews were not the only target of Hitler's despise but they were the most prominent and the most recognizable by the American public, so the shock of the Holocaust began to have an effect. Rarely has a prejudice been so concisely and so horribly staged on such a grand scale. Pictures of Nazi concentration camps reached the public revealing haunting images of skeleton-like prisoners and mountains of rotting corpses. There were stories of grim medical experiments on prisoners, of piles of gold fillings ripped from their mouths, and of lampshades made of their flesh. It was intense and monstrous. The public recoiled at what they recognized as an extreme demonstration of sentiments that they so often found in themselves. This is what comes of unbridled prejudice. People were not only appalled by what the Nazis did, but they were shocked by their own compliance with Nazi thinking. This is what it took to wake people up to the injustice of their discrimination. This is what the Jewish people had to endure in order to be heard.

Among those defamed was the papacy that was said to have knowledge of the holocaust and to have endured it without comment. That silence and the resulting criticism may have motivated Catholic acceptance of the ecumenical principle at the Second Vatican Council of 1962–65. This principle, long promoted among Protestants, reached out to Muslims as well as Jews in a gesture of Catholic friendship that promoted appreciation if not agreement. In 2014 Pope Francis visited Israel and included a tour of the Jewish Memorial to the Victims of Terror, and he prayed at the Western Wall. The Pope does not speak for all Christians, but that visit is a measure of how far the West has come since the peak of religious intolerance during the fifteenth to seventeenth centuries.

The Holocaust might have set an example for others to follow. It might have encouraged anti-Semitism rather than discouraged it. Nazis generally assumed that they were paving the way for future generations. They saw themselves as spearheads of civilization. The Holocaust did in fact present an unambiguous gestalt that could have become the norm because bold undertakings of that kind often do attract a wide following; but thankfully it had the opposite effect in most quarters. The Holocaust placed us at a crossroad between fully accepting or fully rejecting anti-Semitism. There was no longer a dubious in-between, and thankfully the Western world continued in the direction it followed in recent centuries by choosing increased religious tolerance. There is something purposeful about this history. It is possible to believe that there is something about our odyssey on earth that presses us forward along an enlightened path

Of course that claim may sound hollow considering that we have just come through a most violent century. Between the Holocaust and the carpet-bombing of civilians we may seem to have gone backwards. But the aim of war in the twentieth century West has changed somewhat. It is no longer simple conquest and colonization. It results instead in social and economic partnerships as in the case of Germany and Japan after World War II. That was a big step away from plunder and vengeance. Furthermore, we now try to control warfare through international council, however fitful that effort may be. We have also established an international definition of human rights, and we have launched numerous agencies to deal with the deficiency of food and health services around the world. The twentieth century is a curious time of positives and negatives, where it appears that the negatives have often generated the positives. It can be argued that the very harshness of these times has brought fourth our better angles and propelled us in more positive directions. This confused century may yet be seen as another turning point away from the brutality of the ancient world.

THE CIVIL RIGHTS MOVEMENT

Feudalism was a complicated system of rights and privileges that were notably broadened in 1215 when English barons forced King John to sign the Magna Carta extending their rights. England's rise out of feudalism into the modern world is characterized by battles over rights as well as religion. The former reached a peak with the accession of William and Mary on condition of their agreement with the English Bill of Rights. That 1689 act of Parliament laid down limits on the powers of the crown and established the rights of members of Parliament. This and other acts of Parliament coming as late as 1949 are the core of the informal British constitution.

The United States embraced this tradition bag and baggage when the U.S. Bill of Rights was adopted in 1789. This was the name given to the first ten amendments of the U. S. Constitution. These charter documents, including the Declaration of Independence, were the highest expression of eighteenth century enlightenment in that they proclaimed that all men possessed equal rights before God. Of course the word "men" referred to male land-owning Anglicans. It was nonetheless a good show for the eighteenth century.

The most notable and troubling loophole in these documents was the failure to address slavery. The constitutional convention in Philadelphia almost disbanded over that issue. Compromise was found for the moment but the inconsistency could not be indefinitely ignored. The matter of slavery was put aside for another seventy years or so but it finally came to a head.

The American civil war 1861–65 was the most heartbreaking catastrophe experienced by the new republic before or since, and it would have been all the more distressing for America to go through a calamity like that without dealing decisively with the central issue. Following Union victory, a final resolution might still have favored an accommodation to slavery; but fortunately, better heads prevailed. All that sacrifice was not for naught. It might have been easier for Democrats in congress to vote against the 13th Amendment that made slavery unconstitutional, for that would have been consistent with their professed beliefs and with the beliefs of many of their constituents. But just enough of these delegates were persuaded by their highest ideals to vote for the amendment. When the pressure was on to make sense of the war and its great sacrifice, just enough of these delegates saw the point of it all. They not only freed the slaves, they also freed America of its most wrenching inconsistency on the matter of human rights. It is said to be Lincoln's political acumen that enabled this outcome. Perhaps the subjective universe used Lincoln to help those

delegates do their duty, by forcing them to stare into an enlightened gestalt.[2]

The next hundred years were a time of backsliding. After the
high point of the reconstruction amendments, American blacks
sank into a servitude that rivaled slavery in many respects. The Jim
Crow period in the South saw a harsh discrimination against black
people that the rest of the country chose to ignore. Progress is not
linear. The country did not lapse into slavery but we came as close
to it as was legally possible.

ROSA

Rosa Parks was the black woman who refused to give up her bus
seat to a white man in Montgomery Alabama on December 1, 1955,
and was consequently arrested. This sparked the Montgomery bus
boycott and gave Martin Luther King his first notable leadership
opportunity. That in turn generated national interest and kicked
off the ground game of the civil rights movement. There had been
important civil rights developments before this time. Harry Tru-
man integrated the armed forces and the Supreme Court declared
school segregation unconstitutional. But the Montgomery inci-
dent involved blacks successfully rising up on their own behalf,
and it was a turning point in the movement. The people of the
Dexter Avenue Baptist Church and other blacks in Montgomery
were seized by the moment. They were fortunate to have a man
like Martin Luther King on hand to galvanize their cause and
carry them forward. Their outrage spread nationwide to carry us
all forward.

The Jim Crow South was full of barbaric acts that occurred
without apparent response. There were numerous lynching of
blacks and beatings without end. Why didn't any one of these out-
rages trigger a ground swell of resistance? Four months before the
Rosa Parks protest a fourteen-year-old black boy named Emmett
Till was killed in Mississippi for supposedly whistling at a white

2. Goodwin, *Team of Rivals*.

woman. Black indignation may have been widespread but it was not visible to others. Strangely, the offence that spurred blacks to visible action was far less dramatic. It involved a disputed seat on a bus, and Rosa's defiance was not even the first of its kind. Two women did the same thing several months before, and another woman was arrested for the same reason back in 1945.

It is easier to boycott than it is to openly protest because the former is so comfortably anonymous. That may explain why blacks at this time were willing to participate in a bus boycott rather than a lynching protest. Also, the presence of King and other NAACP leadership was a factor. So it was not just Rosa. It was the conjunction of her defiance plus a high quality leadership and the relatively mild nature of the required response. More dramatic sit-ins didn't begin until about five years after Rosa, and the march on Selma didn't occur for another five years after that. But mild as it was, it was the true beginning of the street-level struggle. It inspired a new outlook, a new perspective, and a new hope on the part of blacks. Montgomery sparked a communal change of gestalt: a new understanding of the possible—a revolution. Things like that happen from time to time, and when they do they sprout wings and change history. Its like the cosmos found an opening and dove in.

The Montgomery boycott was one of those events that seem to pop out of nowhere and pulled the nation into it. For almost a century Americans were blind to the lynchings and beatings and other degrading practices in the South, until suddenly they began to see what was happening. The scales began to fall from their eyes but there was a long way to go. There were to be sit-ins and church bombings, freedom rides and assassinations, marches, protests, attack dogs and fire hoses; and in less than ten years the Civil Rights act of 1964 became the law of the land. What a remarkable progression. It was as though the universe suddenly decided that the situation was intolerable and that something had to be done.

The struggle is not finished and may never be finished, but this was a turning point. There will always be racial distinctions among people as well as gender, regional, religious, generational, and class distinctions. Society may minimize these differences or make much of them, but each will always be there and will always be the source of some tension. Ideally, society should minimize these differences and learn to live peacefully with the residue.

The idea being proposed here is that the universe is subjectively purposeful and it calls up fresh gestalts for people to see. It is hard to justify such an idea on the basis of specific events that move history in a positive direction because there are so many events that move history in negative directions. However, it is suggested that the former will overcome the latter in the long run, for our ethical beliefs and practices are superior to those of the ancient world. Supposedly, a conjunction of desire and intelligibility can be expressed through a choice of enlightened gestalts; and the universe thereby places a finger on the scale of positive human development. The Montgomery bus boycott and the freedom trail that followed was one such demonstration.

GAY AND LESBIAN RIGHTS

Harvey Milk was a prominent gay activist who attracted a lot of media attention. He managed to galvanized the gay-lesbian community of San Francisco and beyond in the nineteen seventies. But the rest of the country was little impressed. The same was true of the Stonewall riots that occurred in 1969 in New York's Greenwich Village. A police raid sparked a three-day riot that aroused gays throughout the land, but most of the country regarded the event as a curiosity that had no bearing on themselves. Both Harvey Milk's political career and the Stonewall riot launched the gay-lesbian cause, bringing it to public notice, but what followed was a long gestation period before it really took off.

There were any number of positive developments favorable to LGBT rights between the 1970s and 2005 but public opinion changed little in that time. The Don't Ask Don't Tell policy that is now looked down upon was nonetheless a positive development at the time. It was a necessary step on the way to its repeal. The year 2003 was a banner legal year because the U. S. Supreme Court declared sodomy laws unconstitutional, and the Massachusetts

Supreme Court ruled in favor of gay and lesbian marriage. Still, public opinion remained roughly 50–50 on the question of the legality of sexual relationships between consenting adults.

Then between 2006 and 2013 public opinion shifted dramatically in favor of gay marriage, going from about 27% in 2006 to about 54% in 2013, according to Gallup poles conducted in those years. Maybe the court decisions of 2003 were the cause of this increase. Maybe the large number of friends and relatives coming out of the closet during that time caused a widespread reconsideration of opinion. It isn't clear. Most commentators declare themselves to be baffled by the dramatic increase in approval that occurred over that seven-year period. It is a striking development that is not easily explained. In 2015, Ireland overwhelmingly endorsed gay marriage in a national referendum. That would have been impossible just a few years earlier.

It's as though the public suddenly saw the point. Sexual orientation is like the color of the skin, or the shape of the eyes or nose. It's not the sort of thing you change inasmuch as it's a part of your DNA. How would you like being told to change your sexual preference? Could you do that? Accepting a person's sexual preferences is a matter of good manners and good will. It's a part of the current *zeitgeist* favoring tolerance. People suddenly found a new gestalt, as though the subjective universe abruptly discovered another way to reduce the pain.

VOTING RIGHTS

Not only was slavery overlooked by our founding fathers but they also failed to provide universal voting rights for women, native Americans, Catholics, Jews, Quakers, non-European immigrants, and citizens without property. The separate states were given the power to regulate suffrage and many of them dropped religion and ownership requirements by 1830, but progress toward universal suffrage was measured. States separately adopted amendments giving women the vote beginning with Colorado in 1893, and ending in 1920 with the 19th Amendment to the U.S. Constitution that granted women the nationwide right to vote. Today every citizen of 18 or older has the right to vote, but to this day many barriers to the ballot are still in place for our non-white citizens. As always, it's two steps forward and one step backward.

SOCIAL RIGHTS

There is a second women's movement beginning in 1963 with the publication of Betty Friedan's book on *The Feminine Mystique*. Issues from that time to this day have revolved around the narrow social role allowed to woman—to their place in marriage as wife and child bearer, to discrimination against them in the workplace and before the bench, and to reproductive control of their bodies. There was a concerted effort to enact an Equal Right Amendment to the U.S. Constitution that would ensure women an equal status with men before the law. This effort failed. Nonetheless, the role of women has been expanded considerably since the 1960s. Women are now mayors, governors, CEOs, and presidential candidates. Marriages are now more like partnerships than previously, and the place of women in American society is now far more equitable than it was in the 1950s. If nothing else, the movement has given women a choice. A woman can now choose a more traditional role in the home or in a career outside of the home, or some combination of the two. Women in the 1950s did not seem to have that choice. The failure to obtain an Equal Rights Amendment has slowed the liberating process but it has not been stopped. No doubt it will continue as the century rolls on, as more and more women break away from or simply modify their traditional job descriptions and social roles.

WORKER'S RIGHTS

There is one group that has not benefited from the "rights movement." Workers have not prospered since the 1980s for reasons that are related to the economic atmosphere that has prevailed in the decades since that time. But that's not the only reason. There is something basically wrong with the way workers have asserted their rights—the strike.

When the dockworkers go on strike the whole town shuts down for however long it takes. When the garbage workers go on strike the whole town smells for however long it takes. When a major industry goes on strike the whole country grinds to a halt. The strikers of course lose income for as long as they are out, and the company or industry that is being targeted loses as well. That much is understandable. But why should so many others pay? Why should bystanders become casualties when labor goes to war? Why should a dockworker strike cause everyone pain, and why should everyone in town have to hold his nose when the garbage workers go out?

Workers certainly should have rights to counter the overwhelming power that can be exercised by their employers. For stability in their lives, they need to be able to contract their labor in exchange for a living wage and for sickness and retirement benefits. They can't do that effectively one worker at a time, so they need a union and the ability to bargain collectively. However, they *do not* need the ability to paralyze an entire community with a strike.

When Mr. Jones has issues with his neighbor that cannot be settled by talking it out, he is not left to choose between resignation and violence. He can go to court. He can sue. When the UVWX Corporation has a dispute with another party it does not take to the streets and shoot it out. UVWX goes to court with a civil suit against the party of the second part. That is the accepted way to settle disputes in a civilized society. In doing so, the disputants put themselves in the hands of a judiciary that is knowledgeable of the matters at hand and is not an interested party. The general public is not then involved in the altercation and does not become a combat casualty. That is the way that labor disputes should be settled—not with strikes, but with labor courts.

Presently, the parties to a labor dispute may settle out of court through a process called arbitration. They agree on a third party (an arbitrator) who reviews the case and imposes a decision that is legally binding and enforceable in the courts. If they cannot agree on an arbitrator then the process breaks down. The result is often a strike. Often they don't even look for an arbitrator but go directly to a strike.

I believe that the public, and the workers, and the employers would all benefit if the government at hand "chose" an arbitrator when the parties cannot agree on one, and if the strike as a weapon were made illegal. The country as a whole has shown great sympathy for the rights of others, but they do not seem to extend that concern to the plight of workers. One reason is that workers assert their rights in a way that is primitive—it's an action that does harm to many who are not involved. There are other issues of course, but I believe this is the main reason why a rights-sympathetic public is so detached when it comes to the rights of workers.

ECONOMIC RIGHTS

Human civilization has social, political, economic, and religious dimensions, and there has been substantial Western progress in all of these areas since ancient times. But at the moment America is wallowing in economic doldrums that are accompanied by political dysfunction. We appear to be unwilling to deal with some important economic rights apart from those of labor. What about the rights of all humans (especially children) to three square meals a day? What about the rights of all humans (especially children) to health care and a roof over their heads? There was a time during the twentieth century when there was a vast and prosperous middle class in America, and it was then that President Lyndon Johnson announced a War on Poverty that would fulfill the above rights for all U.S. citizens. For a time it seemed as though we were on the brink of an economic utopia. But somehow it all went wrong. The notion of economic rights in this country has come to a pitiful end, accompanied by a political stalemate that seems to forbid resolution. By the beginning of the twenty-first century the concern of many was focused on saving the middle class, never mind the embattled poor. That downward spiral continues to this day. This issue and the enabling political inaction are addressed in the next chapter.

Question: Many of the claims in this chapter on behalf of cosmic purpose are spotted and indirect—not to mention some contrary indications. Why? Can't more tangible evidence be provided? **Answer**: The evidence is intrinsically indirect. The same is true of many concepts in science We have no direct proof of the Big Bang—only indirect evidence. We have no direct proof of the existence of quarks—only indirect evidence. All of our evidence of the hypothetically constructed objective universe beyond our immediate experience is without direct proof. We take it on faith with the proviso that it is subject to change if a better theory comes along. This applies to the subjective part of the universe as well. In addition, evidence in quantum mechanics is probabilistic, so it sometimes varies widely from the expectation value. In human affairs an in physics, evidence is necessarily indirect *and* probabilistic.

9

DESIRABLE CONFLICTS

LIBERTY AND EQUALITY ARE two fine ideals that are fully worthy of cosmic favor, and yet they conflict with one another. Excessive liberty tends to diminish equality, and excessive equality tends to diminish liberty. Historically, America has gone back and forth between these extremes. Over the years we oscillate between capitalism on the right and socialism on the left, and most of the time we hover somewhere between the two. Either extreme is undesirable because it excludes the other, and any compromise is unclear and unstable. As a result we are always in the mist of a battle between left and right—between liberty and equality. This chapter documents this pendulum swing in America history. It is basically a desirable dialog between two desirable ideas, keeping America on its toes.

The remainder of this chapter is concerned with capitalism and democracy. The first is (or could be) an adequate economic system but the second is a cosmic value on a par with liberty and equality. Neither one of these institutions is presently functioning as it should. I consider how they might be shaped to better serve the public and improve the performance of the pendulum. A proposal is advanced that is designed to improve both.

LIBERTY AND EQUALITY

Many Americans learn at their mother's knee that their country stands for liberty and equality. Many seem to think they are the same thing. But they are *not* the same thing, and in fact, they directly contradict one another. To the extent that liberty reigns, equality is pushed aside; and to the extent that equality reigns, liberty is pushed aside.

Both liberty and equality are ideals that are worthy of cosmic purpose, and both are championed as rights of American citizenship. It was so argued by abolitionists prior to the civil war, and the reconstruction amendments seemed to accomplish that for a time for American blacks. And yet, these two ideas move in opposite directions. One goes to the right and the other goes to the left.

Libertarianism is the ideal on the right and egalitarianism is the ideal on the left. Extreme libertarianism leads to a dominance of an elite, and extreme egalitarianism leads to a dominance of a mediocre mean. When ideologues state their case in favor of one or the other it sounds wonderful because each professes a desirable goal. Liberty is a fine ideal as is equality, but the extreme of each is undesirable because each excludes the other. Each side considers compromise a "slippery slope" in the wrong direction.

Some sort of compromise would seem to be desirable. The trouble is that there is no "ideal" compromise. Libertarianism by itself is ideologically pure and egalitarianism by itself is ideologically pure, but there is no position between them that is ideologically pure. Compromise is intrinsically impure. Not only that, but compromise is intrinsically unstable. If we arrive at an agreement today, then tomorrow there will be pressure to bend the agreement one way or the other.

The American people favor compromise in spite of the messiness of it. They prefer it to extremes. The result is that American politics goes from right to left and back again. There is a pendulum-like oscillation between the two and no one is knows where the middle is located. At any moment there are those on the right who clamor for more liberty, and those of the left who clamor for more equality. This tension results in a constant instability that has driven American politics in cyclic oscillations that last over decades.

The nineteenth century ended with dominance on the right. It was the gilded age when robber barons ran the country. These were the elite who emerged because liberty triumphed over equality. It was however the end of a cycle, for Theodore Roosevelt emerged to oppose the monopolies and to champion a progressive message. This began the first cycle of the twentieth century.

The progressive era lasted until 1920 when Warren Harding led the nation back to normalcy, resulting in the roaring twenties, if that can be called normalcy. This resulted in a right wing expansion that gave the stock market license to go over the top. The business of America, said Calvin Coolidge, is business, and government made no effort to interfere or regulate the growing bubble. This cycle ended in the stock market crash of 1929.

The New Deal began with the election of Franklin Roosevelt in 1932. The thrust of it was to use government to restore balance in the economy. The programs and policies of this era curbed the libertarian spree of business and gave preference to the creation of jobs for the masses. It favored a more equitable distribution of wealth. It was an immensely popular egalitarian move to the left.

The New Deal lasted for forty years until about 1972. There was a brief hiatus until 1980 when Ronald Reagan became president, and at that point the pendulum began a distinct turn to the right where it has been for the past thirty plus years. During this time the emphasis has been on deregulation, destroying unions, and getting the government off the back of business. The tax code has been riddled with loopholes and wages have stagnated. During this time there has been a dramatic redistribution of wealth toward the upper class, while the middle class is saddled with debt and loss of income. The New Deal has been dismantled. We are now way over on the right.[1]

In his book "Our Divided Political Heart," E. J. Dionne discusses a similar pendulum operating in American politics.[2] Instead of a dynamic between liberty and equality, Dionne establishes the dynamic between *individualism* and *the common good*. The result is much the same. He not only describes the above twentieth-century cycles but he goes back to founders like Jefferson and Hamilton. Jefferson championed individualism and Hamilton championed the common good. This assignment may be contrary to the current understanding that associates Jefferson with the Democratic Party and Hamilton with the Republicans on Wall Street, but definitions change over time.

Dionne extends his analysis through the nineteenth century, commenting on the Wigs become Republicans who were then on the left, as opposed to the Democrats who where then on the right. We have throughout our history vacillated between the ideals of liberty and equality (or between individualism and the common good) because these values, however laudable, are dialectically opposed to one another. We cannot have them both in pure form so we have historically fought with ourselves and ended in compromise. That compromise is always unstable and is always on the move, or about to move, from left to right or from right to left.

There is another cyclic movement between the right of investors to a fair profit, and the right of workers to a fair wage. This is a secondary oscillation that follows from and is tethered to the more fundamental clash between liberty and equality. Still another related oscillation is between the dominant corporate interests and the dominate big government.

---

1. I don't mean to suggest that the right-wing agenda is the cause of all of these problems. There are unrelated difficulties like globalization, and as President Obama said: "That ship has sailed." The same is true of improved industrial technology. We cannot reverse these trends by reviving the New Deal. What we need is a Good Deal across the board that can survive globalization and an evolving technology.

2. Dionne, *Divided Heart*.

I believe that this pendulum oscillation is a good thing. In the first place it takes us back and fourth between two good things—liberty and equality, or individualism and the common good. Second, it keeps us on our toes. We would fall asleep politically if we were not occasionally beaten and battered by the necessity to choose between the two. Cosmic purpose appears to be using these two laudable goals as paddles in the political/economic Ping-Pong we play. There is a danger however that we might find ourselves stuck at one extreme for an unbearably long period of time, or stuck in a way that seems to be permanently frozen. That hasn't yet happened but it is possible.

CAPITALISM AND DEMOCRACY

Many say that capitalism is worthwhile in spite of its faults because it delivers great wealth to the greatest number of people. The trouble at the moment is that capitalism is delivering its wealth to a very small number of people—to those who already have it. Capitalism at the moment is not doing its job. Maybe that is because we are at the extreme right of the pendulum swing and the situation will correct itself. Or maybe capitalism has become so entrenched in the political life of the nation that there is no going back. Government is the only sizable opponent of capitalism, which is why the pendulum moves between periods of dominant government and dominant capitalism. If capitalism co-opts government so much that there is no way to shake corporate influence, then the pendulum will be stuck on the right. The middle class will then be permanently disenfranchised.

Fortunately, there is now evidence that the pendulum is beginning to reverse direction.. However, there is reason to believe that the influence of private wealth in government will continue to be excessive because of money in politics, so the pendulum will always execute its oscillations with a bias to the right. This intrinsic right-leaning must be addressed if the pendulum operation is to be smooth, and if timely reversals of direction are guaranteed. Apart from pendulum swings, we must face the issue of how capitalism is destroying our democracy.

There have been many attempts to reform capitalism. The problem according to Richard D. Wolff is that the producers of surpluses and profits (i.e., the workers) are different from the people who obtain and distribute such surpluses and profits (i.e., the capitalist owners). Wolff's solution is to make them the same people. "Workers are to become, collectively, their own board of directors in fully cooperative enterprises." He would make capitalism a co-op.[3] However, it is hard to believe that the *ownership of the means of production* is a cosmic principle in a universe in which ownership is a meaningless idea. In fact, there is a more noble idea that can do the job—democracy.

Apart from the technicality that we use the word democracy to mean representative government, democracy is first-rate institutional cosmic principle. If we applied the democratic principle as intended by our forefathers, the problem of money in government would be reduced to a minor irritation. We do not need to reform capitalism. We need to reform democracy.

It is well documented how money corrupts politics, and it is through this corruption that capitalism excessively skims off profits and leaves the rest of us short-changed. If our representatives in congress and the state legislatures worked more directly for the people they represent, then the excesses of capitalism would be controllable. Capitalism would still not be without fault, but it would then conform more closely to the expectations of the people it serves. It comes down to getting money out of politics, a long-held objective of reformers who seem always to be frustrated by rulings of the courts.

The idea that "money is free speech" first showed up in the Buckley v. Valeo Supreme Court ruling of 1976. It has since become an established legal principle. It is of course ridiculous to say that a person's right to speak is proportional to his wealth. Why not say it is proportional to his waistline or his ability to throw a baseball?

3. Wolff, *Capitalism Hits Fan.*

Rich people will always have an advantage in the market place of ideas. If you are rich, you can buy a radio station, a TV station, or a newspaper or magazine. Or more modestly, you can advertise your opinion on the radio, TV, or in a newspaper, or magazine. If you are rich you have many microphones that you might use to sway public opinion. But to say additionally that wealth has a legal privilege in its own right is the height of absurdity. It sounds medieval. Wealth ought not to have any special political advantage in law, certainly not in a democracy where every man is supposed to be the equal of every other man. Whatever it takes, however hard it may seem to be, we have to get *legally privileged money* out of politics.

There have been many proposals attempting a reform of this kind. A proposal by Laurence Lessig would restrict the amount of money that one could contribute to an office holder.[4] Presumably this would shift the power of money in government from the big guy to the little guy. It would redirect the attention of office holders from the vested interests of the rich and powerful to the concerns of ordinary citizens. It's a good idea but it doesn't go far enough. It still favors one kind of citizen over another. It still gives privileged influence to those who have cash to spare compared to those who are barely able to make ends meet. It still supports the euphemism "political contribution," whose right name is "political bribe."

A vote for an office candidate is not a bribe because it is part of the contract between the candidate and the constituent. The salary paid to the office holder is not a bribe because it is part of the contract between the official and the constituent. However, individual contributions beyond the office holder's salary *are not a part* of the contract. These extra-contractual gifts are intended to solicit special favor—to bribe.

If the mayor of a municipality receives most of his political contributions from the most prosperous part of his town, then his administration will be more inclined to favor that part of town. The same of course will be true if he receives most of his votes from particular precincts; for he is then likely to favor those precincts

4. Lessig, *Republic Lost.*

when it comes to municipal services. However, there is a difference. The former is not contractual, whereas the latter is implicit in the democratic principle. It is unfortunate that those who lose an election will often suffer the consequences, but there is no need to compound this misfortune by allowing a money-based form of favoritism. Extra-contractual money with the respectable name "contributions" is clearly a "bribe" given to the office holder in order to get something in return. That's what it's for, and that's what it does. Continuing this practice even at the diminished rate of the Lessig proposal only sustains bribery at a diminished level.

Of course I too make regular political contributions like so many of my well meaning and law abiding fellow citizens. I tell myself "Everyone does it. I am simply doing what I need to do to be heard." What I am saying is: Political bribery is the norm. I am only defending myself in that situation. From the beginning of the Republic it has been considered virtuous, even patriotic, to bribe officials; so that is what we do. Our forefathers were wrong on this point, and that is why we are cursed with the present prevalence of legally privileged money in politics. I believe that only a more radical reform can rid us of this plague.

Let it be required that persons holding public office or running for public office can only receive material support for themselves or for their campaigns through governments that pay their salaries and underwrite their campaign expenses. It would then be *illegal* for anyone to offer material support to office candidates or office holders or their surrogates, and it would be *equally illegal* for an office candidate or office holder or surrogate to accept any such support. The message to office candidates and holders would then be that their only "boss" is their constituents. Therefore, instead of spending time raising money for their next campaign, they would be able to give their full attention to the needs of those they represent. They can be approached and perhaps persuaded by lobbyists inside or outside of their constituency, but their loyalty would be to those who have voted for them in the past and will potentially vote for them in the future. *Freedom of speech should be widely interpreted to include all forms of communication between individuals and groups of individuals, but that in no way connotes a right to bribe public officials.*

It is true that legislators can be lured by the promise of future employment when they no longer hold office. Most upsetting is when they accept a job lobbying their previous colleagues on behalf of a company or an industry. There is no cure for this behavior except transparency, although that will not completely cushion an office holder from muted suggestions and the temptation of future employment. However, the most compelling influence of lobbyists and other wealthy contributors is the money they put up front *in the present* toward an upcoming campaign. If direct compensation is legally off the table then the influence of lobbyists is likely to be diminished, and companies will be less likely to invest heavily in lobbying efforts. There is then a better chance that legislators will be focused on the needs of their constituents. Office holders now spend a great deal of time and effort raising campaign funds and indebting themselves to special interests. The above proposal would largely free them of that burden and that influence.[5]

Maybe something like this can be achieved by statute if the courts are willing, but it will probably require a constitutional amendment. That effort need not begin at the federal level. Perhaps a few states will begin the amendment process as they did in the case of woman's voting rights. Perhaps some progressive states will get the ball rolling by amending their state constitution to apply to all state office holders and seekers, and maybe to their representatives in the U.S. Congress as well. This would shield all the government officials in the state from the influence of money. Office holders and seekers would then be "reduced to" employees of the people—as our forefathers intended.

---

5. Private money might be spent opposing a candidate or supporting his opponent. To combat this, the candidate should seek support from the government that underwrites his campaign expenses.

Question: Isn't it going too far to say that political contributions to office holders are bribes? **Answer**: When one person pays another for special considerations it is called a bribe. In business relationships, in professional relationships, and among friends, something like that is called a bribe. Only in politics is it thought of as a patriotic virtue. That's why there is so much monetary corruption in our democracy.

LEFT-RIGHT WINGS

The above proposal will not eliminate the periodic pendulum swing from left to right in American politics. There will always be lobbyists and others pushing a point of view. There will always be those on the right who want more liberty and those on the left who want more equality, and this dynamic will insure the kind of instability that results in the pendulum swings previously described. This is not a bad thing. It is a good kind of dialogue and will be even better if legally privileged money is removed from the picture.

It is apparent that my own thinking is over on the left. That's because the pendulum is over on the right. When the ship of state lists starboard, my tendency is to go to port, and when the ship of state lists to port, I go starboard. There is no point standing in the middle like a stick. So if the pendulum does swing to the left, and if (in many years) it has gone too far in that direction, I hope that I (if I'm still around) will have the good sense to recognize the stifling effects of a dominant egalitarianism and become a right-winger.

10

THE EVERLASTING

I CLOSED THE DOOR in chapter 2 on the possibility that consciousness might survive the death of the body. I said that there is no "soul" giving us an everlasting conscious identity in the form of a reincarnated self, or in the form of a lasting repose in heaven. However, the subjective universe proposed in chapter 3 opens a loophole. It allows us to take the notion of reincarnation seriously, although this version of reincarnation does not work the same way as the traditional version.

SPECTRUM OF CONSCIOUSNESS

Different experiences come to us from different parts of the subjective universe. The entire subjective universe is presented to the brains of conscious individuals, but only selected parts of its spectrum are reflected by a particular brain. One brain may reflect pain consciousness, another may reflect joy consciousness, and still another may reflect conscious thought on the subject of geography. The conscious life of an individual is therefore a gathering together of all the spectral components of the subjective universe that are reflected by that person's brain—thereby creating a total conscious experience for that person. Each individual's conscious experience therefore has its origin in a *signature spectrum* that is taken from the full spectrum of the subjective universe, and is peculiar to himself.

When an individual dies his signature spectrum is no longer reflected by his brain, but it might be reflected by the brain of a someone else. In that case, his successor is a kind of reincarnation of the deceased; that is, the successor has the same consciousness, or close to the same consciousness as the deceased. The successor draws his signature spectrum from the same part of the subjective universe as did the deceased.

This is very close to the traditional meaning of reincarnation but it is not the same. Traditionally, the successor is *the same person* as the deceased. Somehow "personhood" jumps the gap between two different bodies—the soul idea again. In the present case however, nothing jumps the gap from one body to the next. Instead, there is a common platform between the two—the subjective universe. Both the deceased and the successor share a similar signature of consciousness that is rooted in the ever-present subjective universe. If a person thinks of his consciousness as something that is peculiar to himself alone, then he and it will die together. But if the person thinks of his consciousness as something that is embedded in a more permanent part of nature, then he will be able to share the everlasting with others.

COINCARNATION

There is no reason why the individual should have to share his signature consciousness with someone in a future generation. He might share it with a contemporary. He might have an "identical twin" in consciousness. Instead of *re*incarnation, this would be *co*incarnation.

Biological twins are never exactly identical because they always have a slightly different history, and so too, *psychic twins* will never be exactly the same because they too will have a slightly different history. You may have a psychic twin on the other side of the world whose values and concerns are surprisingly similar to your own. That person might look very different from you in gender, race, and morphology. He or she might have a different cultural background than your own, and still, there may be a deep commonality between you that is related to your reflecting similar parts of the subjective universe. In fact, you may have hundreds of near-psychic twins throughout the globe at any moment—or thousands, depending on how far you stretch the signature overlap.

You may regard psychic similarities between yourself and these distant and unrecognizable individuals as a DNA fluke, and surely DNA has much to do with who is and who is not a psychic twin. But on the other hand, if you think of these similarities as reflections of the same or similar parts of the enduring subjective universe; then you and your psychic siblings will forever share a connection with the everlasting.

11

KARMA

THE LAW OF KARMA says that persons of good will travel through life with a shield that protects them from evildoers, and those of ill will travel through life as targets of evildoers. The evidence for this law is largely anecdotal. There are too many exceptions. There are too many people like Job who don't seem to deserve what they get, and too many bad guys who get much more than they seem to deserve. Eastern religions account for this discrepancy by righting the balance in another life. It is assumed that Job was bad in a previous life, which is why he suffers in this life; and that any bad person will get his just deserts in the next life. In earlier chapters we denied that karma has an objective significance, but chapter 10 seems to allow that possibility with some modification. As a result, there are two ways for us to understanding karma: one subjective and the other objective.

SUBJECTIVE KARMA

If a person sees the world as friendly, if the glass is half full, then he is not likely to be embittered and vengeful. If he sees the world as unfriendly, if the glass is half empty, then he is more likely to be embittered and vengeful. What matters in Job's case is how he thinks about the way that the world has treated him: glass half-empty or half-full. It matters how he organizes the information of his life into a congenial gestalt or a hostile one. However virtuous his life might have been on the face of it, Job might have harbored malicious thoughts that he projected onto the external world, thereby turning every misfortune into evidence of God's abuse. We will never know. We don't know what enmities Job held in his heart that may have colored his perception; so although there may be substantial outward evidence of his virtues, his subjective goodness is as elusive as the essential badness of Adolf Eichmann.

The problem here is like that of the hurricane. You can put your energy into defending against a hurricane by moving your lawn furniture into the basement and barricading your windows; or you can spend your energy cursing God for your misfortune, or perhaps, cursing the hurricane for its malicious ways. The enlightened man would simply defend himself without bitterness and be grateful for what has been spared. Such a person is not free of disaster but he is free of recrimination and bitterness. It all depends on how one understands what is happening, or how one forms the gestalt. Some will no doubt consider this statement naive. They would say: "You should not fool yourself about what is happening to you. You can't survive in the world without being realistic about your fortunes." That is true. But realism is open to interpretation. The most enlightened person will not survive walking into a rotating blade; but on the other hand, it is not realistic to imagine enemies where there are only flawed people who need to be managed—or at least need to be understood. A great deal can be accomplished by arranging one's reality so that the glass is full, or close to it. Bitterness and vindictiveness can then be avoided. Positive people not only make the world more pleasant for themselves, but they do the same for everyone around them.

This describes the *Law of Karma* as a subjective principle. It says that persons of good will travel through life with a positive view of events, and that persons of ill will travel through life with a negative view of events. So the question is: Does the subjective universe have a stake in this idea? It would seem so. We have seen that the subjective universe wants to maximize the pleasure and minimize the harm done to humans, and it does this by encouraging more humane attitudes between human beings, and fostering more humane institutions in the social life of humans. It does this by bringing forward gestalts whenever possible that achieve these objectives.

OBJECTIVE KARMA

On the other hand, there is an objective version of the karmic principle. In the previous chapter we learned that we share our part of the subjective universe with many others—our psychic siblings. That similarity may manifest itself in a common objective behavior, so our psychic siblings might also be our behavioral siblings. Those who think and behave in similar ways often recognize one another. They congregate together and do similar things with and to one another. This may very well be the theoretical basis of an objective law of karma. Criminal types best understand each other and tend to associate together. This may be because they share a common background, or because they share a same way of looking at the world independent of background. For whatever reason, they are psychic siblings who interact with one another, and who *do to each other* what criminals *do onto others*. In that circle, what goes around comes around.

So it is with any circle of like-minded people. An objective law of karma can therefore be established on the basis of a shared subjective universe that manifests itself objectively.

12

AND BEYOND

————————

WE HAVE DEFINED COSMIC purpose to derive from tendencies of the subjective universe to bring forth enlightened gestalts among individuals. We now give voice to the possibility that a purposeful subjective universe might have existed in other forms.

OTHER UNIVERSES

The current proposal in figure 4 of chapter 6 reduces to figure 5 during the 13 billion years or so between the Big Bang and the time of the first introduction of brains. It shows the objective universe and the subjective universe as being complementary to one another, where anchor and nonanchor forces are not yet present because there are no conscious brains present. In that case, the subjective universe would be made up entirely of the undifferentiated elements of consciousness that have not yet been reflected by a brain. The two halves in the figure are interactive, making a single monistic universe. This universe is not purposeful during this evolutionary era because our definition of cosmic purpose does not apply without brains to give it definition.

Objective Universe | Subjective Universe

Figure 5. A possible early universe

We now suppose that the universe during this time *is* purposeful. Purpose must then be defined differently because our definition of cosmic purpose will not survive an epoch without differentiated conscious images. This idea is suggested by the fact that the early universe seems to have conspired to create conscious organisms, and that is the *only* evidence. That is thin testimony for such a bold idea. It suggests that the subjective universe had an equal status with the objective universe from the beginning, and that it guided the evolution of the objective universe in a way that assured the emergence of conscious creatures. It's a tempting idea. But apart from the scant evidence, it is difficult to imagine a narrative that would carry this model to the point of plausibility.

More dramatically, and more likely, there are current speculations about multiple universes. The choices include universes with different laws and different physical constants than our own, and it is unlikely that conscious organisms can be sustained in all of these cases. It is commonly imagined that all possible multiple universes coexist with our own because *if something can happen it will happen*. It is therefore supposed that our universe with its ability to create consciousness just happened to appear among all of the "inert" possibilities—including the ones that are like our own but never caught fire.

THE FOUR-PART MODEL

The most promising possibility is the four-part model of chapter 6, or at least, it is the most easily understood. We have so far developed "purpose" in terms of a cosmic desire to maximize pleasure and minimize pain, where this is accomplished by the exercise of cosmic free-will to support existing gestalts or create new ones. This choice is objectively carried out with nonanchor forces.

This rather limited scenario only raises the question as to what other purpose a four-part universe might pursue. It is hard to imagine the full extent of a cosmic purpose because we don't know what the universe has in mind, but one might wonder: In what other way might the universe want to use conscious beings? Does it only want to look around and admire itself with our eyes, avoiding pain and realizing pleasure wherever possible? Does it only want to build tall buildings with our hands? Does it want to wage war on itself using our lunacy? Does it want all of these things in a colossal contest between good and evil? Or is it possible that the universe just wants to use conscious beings in order to observe and understand itself, deriving pleasure from that alone like a cosmic Socrates. On the other hand, Toyohiko Kagawa says that we cannot know the purpose of universal evolution until its final unfolding, as though purpose has only to do with the end-game.[1]

These ideas take us further than this book is prepared to go. It is better to stick to the more modest four-part proposal that has been developed so far. Of course, within that model there are alternative structures as was pointed out in Chapter 7. Maybe the subjective universe has a super brain after all, and maybe it has an ability to create gestalts of its own. Maybe it independently plans ahead and develops a purposeful strategy that it imposes on the conscious creatures in its domain. Maybe! But this is another way of introducing God into the works. It's another way of saying that we humans were put into the universe to serve(to some extent) the wishes of an overlord.

Contrary to this, the thesis of this book is that we were introduced to serve as the eyes and ears of the universe, and it is through us that the universe takes on a purposeful direction. This human-based scenario does not endow the subjective universe with separate and controlling god-like capabilities. It is a narrative that places humans in the forefront, allowing our species to use the

1. Kagawa *Cosmic Purpose*

subjective universe to direct the flow of history toward our long-term well-being.

Question: Doesn't one need to posit the existence of God in order to explain the existence of the entire universe? **Answer**: If you posit the existence of God to explain the existence of the universe, then you have to explain the existence of God. If you say that God was created by something called Po, then you have to explain the prior existence of Po. And if you say that Po was created by something called Quo, then you have to explain the prior existence of Quo—and so forth. I'm afraid we are stuck with an existence that is basically inexplicable. There is no absolute prior cause that we can know about. All we can do is describe the internal consistency of what we have.

An agnostic says he does not know about the existence of God—understood as an absolute prior cause. I say we *cannot know* about a prior cause; or if we do, it becomes an internal cause. So if there is a cosmic purpose in our universe it must be generated within the universe—consistent with and logically related to the other parts of the universe. This is what has been done in this book.

BIBLIOGRAPHY

Bob, Petr. *Brain, Mind, and Consciousness*. New York: Springer, 2011.

Carlson, Neil R. *Physiology of Behavior*. Boston: Allyn & Bacon, 2010.

Chalmers, David J. *The Conscious Mind*. Oxford: Oxford University Press, 1996.

————. *The Character of Consciousness*, Oxford University Press, Oxford 2010

Clifford, William. "Body and Mind." In *Lectures and Essays*, edited by Leslie Stephen and Frederick Pollock. London: Macmillan, 1886.

Crick, Frances H. C., and Christof Koch. "Towards a Neurobiological Theory of Consciousness." *Seminars in The Neuroscience 2* (1990) 263–275.

Dennett, Daniel. *Consciousness Explained*. Canada: Little-Brown, 1991.

Dennett, Daniel and Marcel Kinsbourne. "Time and the Observer: the Where and When of Consciousness in the Brain." *Behavior and Brain Science 15* (2) (1992) 183–247.

Dionne, Eugene J. *Our Divided Political Heart*. New York: Bloomsbury, 2012.

Donderi, Don C. "Visual Complexity: A Review." *Psychological Bulletin 132 No. 1* (2006) 73–97.

Eagleman, David M. "How does the Timing of Natural Signals Map onto the Timing of Perception." In: *Space and Time in Perception and Action*, edited by R. Nijhawan and B. Khurana, Cambridge: Cambridge University Press, 2010.

Engel, Andreas K., et al. "Temporal Binding, Binocular Rivalry, and Consciousness" *Consciousness and Cognition 8* 1999.

Gawande, Atul. *Being Mortal*. New York: Henry Holt, 2014.

Goodwin, Doris K. *Team of Rivals: The political Genius of Abraham Lincoln* New York, Simon & Schuster 2005

Heylighen, Francis. "Complexity and Self-Organization." *Encyclopedia of Library and Information Sciences*, ed: Marcia Bates and Mary Maack. New York: CRC, 2009.

Hobbes, Thomas. *Leviathan (1651)*. Oxford: Oxford University Press, 1996.

Hofstadter, Douglas R. and Daniel C. Dennett. *The Mind's I: Fantasies and Reflections on Self and Soul*. New York: Basic, 1981.

Kagawa, Toyohiko. *Cosmic Purpose*. Portland: Cascade, 2014.

Kristof, Nicholas, and Sheryl WuDunn. *A Path Appears—Transforming Lives, Creating Opportunities.* New York: Alfred A. Knopf, 2014.

James, William. "The Principles of Psychology, Vol. 1." In *The Works of William James*, edited by F. Bowers and I, K. Skrupskelis. Cambridge: Harvard University Press, 1975.

Lessig, Lawrence. *Republic Lost.* New York: Hachette, 2012.

Locke, John. "Essays Concerning Human Understanding (1689)." In *The Empiri-cists*, abridged by Richard Taylor, 100–101. New York: Random House, 1961.

Merali, Zeeya. "This Quantum Life." *Discover Magazine 35(10)* (December 2014) 44–49.

Mould, Richard A. "Evolution of Consciousness I." *Activitas Nervosa Superior 51:2* (2009) 81–86.

———. "Evolution of Consciousness II." *Activitas Nervosa Superior 51:1* (2009) 87–89.

———. "Evolved Consciousness." *Activitas Nervosa Superior 52:3-4* (2010) 141–145.

Nagel, Thomas. "What is it Like to be a Bat?" *Philosophical Review 83* (1974) 435–450.

Nietzsche, Friedrich. *Beyond Good and Evil.* Oxford: Oxford University Press, 2008.

O'Regan, J. Kevin and Alva Noë. "A Sensorimotor Account of Vision and Visual Consciousness." *Behavioral and Brain Sciences 24* (2001) 939–1031.

O'Regan, J. Kevin. *Why Red Doesn't Sound Like A Bell.* Oxford: Oxford University Press, 2011.

Pinker, Steven. *The Better Angles of our Nature: Why Violence has Declined?* New York: Penguin, 2012.

Rose, James D. "The Neurobehavioral Nature of Fishes and the Question of Awareness and Pain." *Reviews of Fisheries Science 10(1)* (2002) 1–38.

Singer, Wolf "Consciousness and the Binding Problem." *Annals of New York Academy of Sciences 929* (2001) 123-146

Von Neumann, John. *Mathematical Foundations of Quantum Mechanics.* Princeton: Princeton University Press, 1955.

Wolff, Richard. *Capitalism Hits The Fan.* Northampton MA: Olive Branch, 2013.

INDEX